Praise For
Breathing Oxygen

"Positive leadership and positive cultures are needed more than ever. There are people who breathe life into every relationship, room, and team, and also those who steal the oxygen and energy. Thanks to Jason for breathing good oxygen into others!"

Jon Gordon
Twelve-time bestselling author of *The Energy Bus* and *The Power of Positive Leadership*

"Servant Leadership is about giving energy and care to others and a mission greater than self. The best cultures breathe oxygen into the mindsets of their people in alignment with their values. Jason Barger's work and spirit continue to give energy to me and countless teams in the world."

Howard Behar
Former president, Starbucks Coffee

"Behaviors such as agility, grit, empathy, and inclusivity have never been more essential and more valued in the workplace. Jason Barger's six key mindsets highlight the behaviors that propel great leaders and drive great cultures."

Coley O'Brien
Chief people officer, The Wendy's Company

"Every winning team breathes in good oxygen that fuels their mindsets and culture. Many losing teams share too much toxic air of blame, selfish pursuits, or excuses. It starts with a choice that every individual and every leader makes. Jason Barger's message is refreshing and needed to build healthy teams."

Shane Battier
Two-time NBA champion

"Culture and values are the air we breathe. They are things we never stop working on, developing, and sharing with each other. Jason Barger is on target again that leaders and all associates breathe life into winning cultures!"

Cameron Mitchell
Founder, Cameron Mitchell Restaurants

"It's clear from the research that meaningful cultures don't just magically happen. They are co-created by leaders and people who breathe intentional oxygen into their habits, practices, structures, and operations. Jason Barger's insights for developing leaders and cultures are foundational!"

Tamara Myles
Author, speaker, and researcher

"Positive cultures lift each other up and are able to be honest and authentic, seek possibilities, and exhibit grit to find solutions. The best teams are vulnerable with each other and still find optimism for the future. Thank you, Jason!"

Jeni Britton
Founder of Jeni's Splendid Ice Creams

"The mindsets we breathe every day as human beings impact the people and leaders we become in our organizations and in the world. To become more inclusive and accountable to one another, breathing good oxygen is critical. Thank you, Jason Barger!"

Kevin Clayton
VP of diversity, equity and inclusion,
The Cleveland Cavaliers Companies

"The Latin definition of inspire is 'to breathe life into,' which is exactly what Jason's latest leadership masterpiece *Breathing Oxygen* will do for your business, your team, and your life. Prepare yourself for a journey of personal and professional transformation."

Paul Epstein
Former NFL and NBA executive
and bestselling author of *The Power of Playing Offense*

"Creating cultures of inclusivity, grit, and ownership that lift people up and make us all better is needed. Our job as leaders is to breathe good oxygen into ourselves and everyone around us. Jason's message and work are contagious in the good ways!"

Ken Bouyer
Director of inclusive recruiting (Americas), EY

"Employee engagement is a direct response to feeling loved, respected, valued, and supported. Thriving cultures are committed to supporting life-affirming environments where people can do their best work. Breathing in this good oxygen makes everything healthier, better, and more resilient."

Lachandra Baker
Senior director of employee engagement and DEI,
National Church Residencies

"Jason highlights the key leadership mindsets behind every significant impact that is made in the world by individuals, teams, organizations, and communities: clarity, inclusivity, agility, grit, rest, and ownership. As Jason shares, our mindsets and actions impact everything."

Doug Ulman
President and CEO, Pelotonia

www.amplifypublishing.com

For more information, please contact:
Amplify Publishing, an imprint of Mascot Books
620 Herndon Parkway, Suite 320
Herndon, VA 20170
info@amplifypublishing.com

Cover Design: Adam Emery

Library of Congress Control Number: 2021920765

CPSIA Code: PRV0222A

ISBN-13: 978-1-63755-232-2

Printed in the United States

This book is dedicated to every person along my path who has breathed oxygen into me. I'm grateful for the family, friends, strangers, mentors, colleagues, teams, and inspiring leaders along my path who, whether they knew it or not, fueled me. Your words, spirit, commitment, and action expanded my lungs and sustained my journey. Thank you. You've helped shape my mindset, which has impacted my actions. I'm especially grateful for my wife, Amy, and our children, who breathe oxygen into me daily. May we all continue to expand our awareness, capacity, connection, and action in the world. I'm grateful for the good air I've been lucky to breathe.

BREATHING OXYGEN

How Positive Leadership
Gives Life to Winning Cultures

JASON V. BARGER

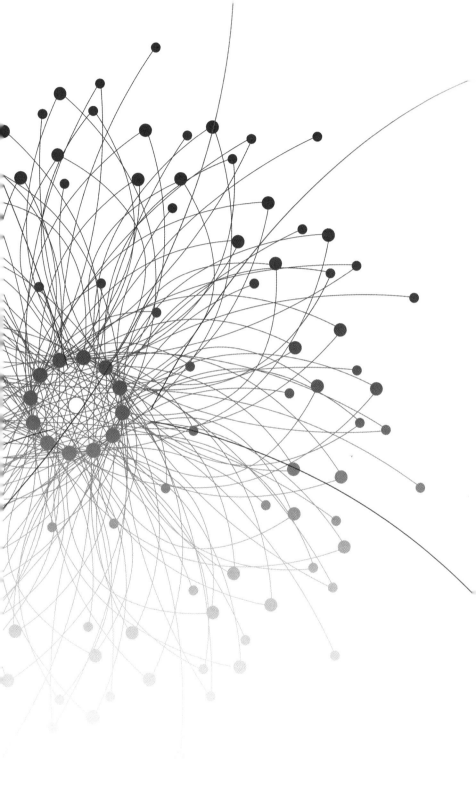

WHY I WROTE THIS BOOK

Every word in this book is true for my own life.

When I consume positive, healthy, good air, my energy and performance expand.

When I consume negative, unhealthy, toxic air, my energy and performance deflate.

The air we breathe is everything. I need to breathe in good air. I need oxygen to help fuel my mind, my heart, and my response to the world around me. I'm guessing you do too.

We are in times of rapid change, division between people, and uncertainty happening all around us—so much that seems out of our control. In all times, the air we breathe, the mindsets we fuel, and the actions we contribute are everything.

I've also witnessed this within the leadership teams and organizations I research, study, and personally serve around the globe.

When leaders and teams consume positive, healthy, good air, their energy and performance expand. The alignment of their mission, vision, and values is palpable. They are ambassadors for their culture every single day and consistently set the temperature for the culture they desire for tomorrow. The oxygen they breathe fuels them individually and collectively.

When leaders and teams consume negative, unhealthy, toxic air, their energy and performance deflate. It leads to wasted energy from fighting mental viruses of negativity, blame, doubt, power, and control. Alignment is broken. The mission is lost. The vision is blurry. Values are sacrificed for personal gain or venomous control. It is as if mental poison is being digested, and the culture corrodes because of it.

There are oxygen givers and oxygen takers. It's a choice we all make with each room we walk into—will we give oxygen to the room or take oxygen from it?

None of us is perfect. Both of these outcomes are possible realities for every human, leader, and group of people on the planet. And we often move between healthy and unhealthy on a spectrum.

The key is to understand and choose the good air to breathe. What air expands, and what air deflates?

What do we choose to inhale, and what do we choose to exhale? Both are important.

What sustains and gives life to our mind, our heart, and our actions, and what strangles and suffocates us and those around us?

I wrote this book because I'm trying to live the spirit of this mindset daily. It helps me be the best version of me. I also wrote it because I'm committed to engaging the minds and hearts of people. I wrote it because I help support the development of leaders and cultures. I wrote it because I see a direct causation between our daily mindsets (the air we breathe) and our effectiveness in our life and work.

We are all leaders in some sense. And because of that, it's important for us to define this word "leadership" from the beginning, because it is a word that has been hijacked over the years. Many people use the term leadership loosely and regularly but do not ever define what authentic and compelling leadership truly looks like. Many people in roles of leadership have also modeled divisive and self-serving behaviors that do not represent true leadership that is compelling, inspiring, and galvanizing. So, the term "leadership" becomes blurry for many and can become hijacked because it is focused on control, power, and the needs of a few. This isn't leadership.

When a leader sees themselves at the "top of the pyramid" and thinks their role as a leader is to bark out orders as the general or dictator, then that is the way they enter every room. Every discussion, decision, or interaction is about power and control. It's also easy for complacency to set in with this kind of mindset because the person believes they've "earned" their way to the top and are protected. How we see what it means to be a leader impacts how we show up. For many, unfortunately, this is the image they grew up with or was modeled for them. They get tricked into thinking this is leadership. It is not.

True, authentic, compelling, and influential leadership gives energy to others rather than takes it. Authentic servant leaders, even if they are at the top of the organizational or hierarchical pyramid based on their role, don't see themselves that way. They don't see their role as a leader as being to sit at the top and bark out orders to those down below. They flip the pyramid upside down in their own mind and, more importantly, their own heart. They see their role as a leader as being at the bottom of the pyramid and serving others, putting others into positions to be successful, and focusing on a mission greater than self. Because this is how they see what it means to be a leader, it impacts how they enter every room, every conversation, and every interaction. It's the air they breathe.

This leadership spirit is committed to the growth of others and helps all contribute to an outcome that couldn't be experienced or achieved alone. It is not about exerting and showing people an example of power but about the power of an example that emerges when someone serves the needs of the whole. Leaders connect. Serve. Paint a vision. Empower collective ownership. Align people.

Over the past decade, I have had the extreme pleasure of speaking and consulting with teams, companies, associations, and organizations across the globe. Throughout the United States, Latin America, Asia, and the Middle East, I have asked a consistent question to an estimated seventy thousand people over the years. The question is, "What are the characteristics of the most influential, compelling, and exceptional leader you have ever experienced or witnessed in your life and career?" Do you know how many times in all those years they answered the question in a way that pointed to a top-of-the-pyramid kind of leader?

Zero.

Not once in all those years and with all those people has anyone stood up and named the attributes of a top-of-the-pyramid leader as the best example. Every single time they describe the attributes of a bottom-of-the-pyramid leader who is clearly on a mission greater than self. They describe someone who is empathetic and trustworthy, a listener, a coach, and a creative and adaptable collaborator. They paint an image of a person who is relentless in finding solutions to positively transform the mission and those on the journey.

If you've been on this journey with me and followed the narrative of this work that I've been lucky to serve for the last twenty-two-plus years, then I'm glad you're here. You'll quickly see how the messages of my previous books have not only mirrored my own development and the continuation of this work but how all the messages build upon each other. My first book, *Step Back from the Baggage Claim*, speaks to the power of stepping back to gain personal perspective and reflecting on how we want to move through the world. *ReMember* is an invitation to renew our priorities, relationships, and focus in a distracting world. *Thermostat Cultures* is about *how* proactive leaders and teams strategically shape the culture they want rather than just the reactionary culture they experience. And now, *Breathing Oxygen* is about six leadership mindsets and actions that help fuel, sustain, and keep that culture going. I'm continuously honored, humbled, and grateful that the books have resonated with so many. If you're new to this conversation, welcome.

Some of us are leaders by title, but most are leaders by the sheer reality that someone is watching the way we move throughout our life and work and is taking cues from how we respond. We are influencing them. We are setting a temperature for them. We are modeling for them what it means to be a leader. They are looking to others for direction, support, and clarity for how they should respond next. I've experienced the power within groups of people (teams, families, friends, communities, entire organizations, and nations) when there is clarity on the type of leaders we are aiming to be and collective ownership for *how* we show up together. We're always creating culture with those around us.

From the beginning of this book, I also want us to understand what I mean by the words *positive* and *winning* that show up in the subtitle of this book. Positive leadership is not about blindly staying upbeat and ignoring the challenges we are facing just because we are trying to stay "positive." Positive leadership is about being honest, open, and transparent about the challenges we are facing and still choosing to be optimistic about the role we play in creating a better future. Positivity is about believing in our response to help move things forward and make things better. Also, a winning culture is about more than just winning the contest, becoming best in class, or the best at what you do (although I hope for that too). A winning culture is one that is authentic to the culture you want to create. Winning is when we accomplish a mission in alignment with the values we hold. Positive leadership gives life to winning cultures.

We all have the ability to breathe oxygen into ourselves. We all have the ability to breathe oxygen into others. It requires intentionality with the mindset we choose as leaders and the actions we put into practice. Let's be intentional about the mindsets and actions we breathe life into.

We need it. Our teams need it. Our world needs it.

Let's breathe oxygen together.

THE CASE FOR DEVELOPING LEADERS AND CULTURE

Over the past two decades, I've experienced this same phenomenon throughout small businesses, sports teams, nonprofit organizations, and Fortune 100 companies.

Either a team believes in the irrefutable power of compelling leadership and the galvanizing spirit of the culture of *how* things are implemented rather than just *what* is done, or they believe that is just fluff. A team with the fluff mindset believes that the success of any entity is just made up of people performing individual jobs with their heads down. The *how* is irrelevant.

If you are of the fluff mindset, then I invite you to stick with this conversation, because I do hope you'll come to the other side. But I'm also realistic; this just might not be for you. I'm okay with that. I've realized over the past twenty years that someone who wants to stay in that mindset is often comforted by that line of thinking. That is the air they choose to breathe.

My observation, however, is that while those types of leaders and teams may achieve a certain level of measured success, the culture within their teams and organizations feels soulless over time. I don't say that with any sense of judgment, just observation. There isn't a galvanizing spirit or heartbeat of the team and organization that compels people to be attracted to that group, stay within it, or develop anything beyond their individual tasks. They go to work and then go home. In many ways, they are comforted by that or have never experienced anything more.

Fortunately, I've found that the overwhelming majority of people in the world do believe in and have experienced the irrefutable energy of authentic leadership and the galvanizing spirit of a compelling team culture. They have experienced either the deflating impact of a soulless leader, coach, or boss that corrodes any sense of chemistry within a team, or they've experienced the life-giving energy from a leader, coach, or mentor that breathes oxygen into all around them. They've been on a team that was extremely talented but could never figure out why they continued to underachieve, or they've experienced the euphoric feeling of being a part of a unified team that seemingly achieves way more than they thought was humanly possible.

The examples are all around us. Just scan the landscape of business, sports, social enterprise, or community organizing. Those that are alive with authentic and participatory leaders and culture are thriving.

If you haven't figured out by now, I believe wholeheartedly in the role that authentic leadership and compelling cultures play in creating anything of significance in the world. Nothing great has ever been accomplished without conscious leadership and the collective spirit of a team culture focused on a mission greater than self.

Developing leaders and culture is the sustaining oxygen of every group of people on the planet. Either it expands their abilities and what is possible, or it deflates and corrodes. Either they breathe oxygen into themselves and others, or they take it away.

But don't just take my word for it. Let's allow research and data to chime in.

There has been extensive research on trends over the last decade about the future of work, conscious capitalism, and the growing desire people have for meaningful work. These studies and research point to the fact that people don't just want a job; they want to be a part of something greater than self and contribute to a culture.

University of Pennsylvania researchers Wesley Adams and Tamara Myles studied various-sized "exemplar" companies and organizations (Google, Zappos, HubSpot, KPMG, Marriott, Nutanix, and BetterUp, to name just a few) who have been lauded for leadership and culture that lead to meaningful work environments.

"Meaningful work" in their research is defined as "work that an individual subjectively believes to be significant, advances toward a desired goal, and contributes to something greater than the self."

As I spoke with Wesley and Tamara about this important and groundbreaking study, one thing became painfully obvious to us all: none of the findings were surprising.

They spoke about the excitement that came from their effort to dive into this new frontier of work and discover the holy grail— the secret sauce, the missing piece that nobody had ever found or thought of. Instead, they found overwhelming evidence that the "secret sauce" was not secret at all. In fact, it was many of the same tenets of leadership development and culture-shaping that we've known for years. It isn't rocket science.

The data revealed that ten principles of meaningful work rise to the surface. Principles like the clarity necessary when hiring the right person. The power of first impressions and onboarding. Managers who walk the walk and talk the talk as role models. And team ecosystems in which everyone participates in the company culture, to name just a few. (Please see the resources in the back of the book to dive into the full study.)

But what was abundantly clear in their findings is that the problem isn't that we don't know these foundational pieces of leadership and culture; it's that they aren't widely practiced. They are known but not lived. Leaders are not breathing oxygen into their teams and organizations consistently with the foundational elements of developing leaders and culture.

The research also pointed out that there is tremendous opportunity and need for stronger leadership and more meaningful cultures. The data shows that people are thirsty to be a part of meaningful work in partnership with compelling leaders and cultures.

Nine out of every ten people say they would take a pay cut to have a job with more meaning, according to a 2018 poll of over two thousand people included in Wesley and Tamara's research.

Add that data to Gallup's robust research over the years focused on employee engagement trends that show employee engagement hovers around 33 to 36 percent. They define "engaged" in their employee data as "those who are highly involved in, enthusiastic about, and committed to their work and workplace."

Around 13 percent of employees are "actively disengaged," which means about 54 percent of workers are "not engaged" and are "psychologically unattached to their work and company."

What does this all mean? It means there is tremendous work to be done and opportunity to engage your people. They want to be engaged. They want to be a part of something. They want to contribute and have meaning.

Why do some teams with basically the same level of talent as their competitors succeed, while others fall short?

Why do some businesses seem to capture the minds and hearts of their employees, while other similar organizations simply sputter along?

Why do some relationships, marriages, or families seem to thrive in the midst of busy schedules and challenging situations, while others become scattered and splintered?

Leadership and culture.

No matter what they are doing, *how* they do it is different. They have clarity and alignment that allow them to adapt, grow, and develop. Not because they are perfect (none of us are) but because they are committed to a vision of a greater future, together.

I hope you'll read this book because you want to play a role in creating compelling cultures in your life and work. You want to bring out the best in yourself and others. You know deep down that everything will be better because of the mindset you fuel and the culture you create as a leader.

You know it's easier to not care, to disengage, and to go back into autopilot mode in your life and career. But in your most honest moments, you know you desire more.

Let's breathe oxygen into ourselves and those around us.

CHAPTER 1

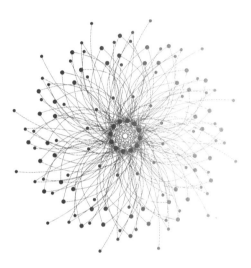

BREATHING OXYGEN
Mindsets That Expand

Breathing (noun)—The process of moving air into and out of the lungs to facilitate gas exchange with the internal environment, mostly to bring in oxygen and flush out carbon dioxide.

Breathing Oxygen (this book's definition)—The process of cultivating the mindsets and actions that fuel energy, possibility, connection, and progress while flushing out negativity, blame, and toxins. The fuel that facilitates positive change that begins internally and flows to the external environment.

"When you get up to a certain elevation on Mount Everest, the air changes."

Those words from Andy Politz, who participated in numerous search-and-rescue missions on Everest for years, still echo in my mind. His description of the thin air at high altitudes and the "four breaths" it requires to accomplish any task has stuck with me. I can hear the four deep and slow inhales of the oxygen of each voyager in order to propel one more step of their snow-covered boot. Four breaths and another step. Four breaths. Step. Four breaths. Step. At that elevation, that is what is required. You've got to breathe very intentionally. In clear scientific terms, a greater volume of air must be inhaled at altitude than at sea level in order to breathe in the same amount of oxygen in a given period.

Humans typically take about twenty-five thousand breaths per day, and some days are more challenging than others. The air has been very thin at many altitudes over the years. As I type this, we are coming out of a global pandemic that has now claimed nearly five million lives worldwide to date (and growing). In the United States, civil unrest, racism, and political and economic uncertainty have challenged us all. Divorce rates are up 34 percent year over year, and the CDC reported that in June 2020, 11 percent of adults in the United States seriously considered suicide. To say things have been challenging would be an understatement. Division, blame, and negativity swirl, while others seek solutions, connection, and personal accountability. The need for strong mental health has been as noticeable as ever. Every human on the planet flows through times of good mental health and struggling mental health. It's a spectrum. Four breaths are required. How we breathe impacts the step we take next.

Some teams, organizations, and businesses have experienced extreme hardship, uncertainty, and loss. Others have seen opportunities emerge to connect, grow, and experience success beyond what they thought was possible. No matter which altitude you are experiencing on your journey, your mindset and how you breathe matter.

This book is focused on those who want to exhale the negativity, blame, and toxic divisive rhetoric. This book is for those of us who want to practice fueling our minds and daily actions with air that expands our abilities rather than deflates them. This book is for

those of us who know we need good oxygen for the jourr
know our ability to breathe oxygen into others as well wiii make
all the difference.

Oxygen and brain function are critical. Without enough oxygen, the brain has trouble signaling where to send blood to oxy-
gen-starved muscles and tissues. Fueled by this oxygen, the brain
coordinates thought, emotion, behavior, movement, and sensation.
Oxygen fuels the four lobes of the brain (frontal, parietal, occipital,
and temporal) that serve the main body functions. Functions like
thinking and problem-solving, planning, and short-term memory
(frontal); sensory information like taste, touch, and temperature
(parietal); processing of images and stored information for memory
(occipital); and the processing of smell, taste, and sound information
in our memory (temporal).

The brain actively uses about 25 percent of the oxygen we take
in to supply the necessary organs and functions. When the brain
doesn't receive enough of the oxygen that it needs, then cerebral
hypoxia (or starvation) sets in. This leads to things like poor judgment, uncoordinated movement, and a decline in cognitive abilities.
In more severe situations, it can lead to stroke, poisoning, choking,
cardiac arrest, or respiratory failure.

The oxygen we breathe is crucial to our existence but also to
our level of functionality and performance and our ability to think
and respond to all that is happening around us.

Higher-quality air will enhance our functionality.

Lower-quality air will starve and poison our functionality.

So, which air do we choose to breathe?

According to the National Science Foundation, an average person has about twelve thousand to sixty thousand thoughts per day.
Of those, 80 percent are identified as negative thoughts, and 95
percent are repetitive thoughts. The research shows that the most
common patterns of negative thoughts are regrets of the past, fear of
the future, unhealthy comparisons with others, and blame. Studies
show that we spend much of our days doing mental gymnastics
around false narratives of a future that hasn't happened yet or of

debilitating comparisons. Following these mental pathways makes it harder to breathe, not easier.

I also observe it within teams and organizations I support. When there is a void in healthy communication in a relationship, within a team, or across an entire organization, the void is often filled by fear, gossip, finger-pointing, and false information. Toxic air spreads. The healthiest teams are the ones who don't let too much time pass without intentionally filling the air and developing mindsets around clarity, inclusivity, agility, grit, rest, ownership, and ultimately hope.

Here ends the scientific portion of the book about the actual chemical element that we call oxygen. In the same way that the chemical fuels the functionality of our entire body, so do the mindsets and actions that we experience each day. Our brains and the oxygen we take in (thoughts, stories, focus, and mindset) impact how we see, experience, and perform in the world.

For years, researchers have been studying and sharing with us the power of our minds and thoughts. Psychologists have shown us the power (and positive impact) of having a growth mindset versus a fixed mindset. A growth mindset sees the world through a lens where every person and situation can grow as a result of learning, effort, and persistence. A fixed mindset sees the world through a lens where everything is already carved in stone. The person and situation are finite. One mindset gives oxygen, and another one tends to take oxygen out of the room.

The famous positive psychologist Dr. Martin Seligman shared how his research on positive psychotherapy helped people overcome depression, "not only by reducing its negative symptoms but also by directly and primarily building positive emotions, character strengths, and meaning."

The UC Davis Medical Center lists twelve benefits of a grateful mindset, ranging from reduced stress and a reduction in inflammation in patients with congenital heart disease to a 10 percent improvement in sleep quality in patients with chronic pain, 76 percent of whom had insomnia, and 19 percent lower depression levels. People seen as grateful are found to generally be happy and have more social connections and fewer bouts of depression. People seen as having a more negative mindset generally experience more toxic and volatile challenges.

It's not just a matter of "thinking positively" but a connection between the mindset, vision, and action that follow. All of this is founded in research but comes alive for us all when our own experiences, stories, and actions are shared.

In words that I've shared in other books, where you look is where you go! What we give our minds and hearts to is where our bodies follow. What gets our focus, our attention, our thoughts, and our hearts is where we go. You're taught this when you learn to surf or ski or ride a motorcycle. What gets your eyes is where your body will follow. Our minds are no different. If what gets your attention is negativity, gossip, blame, and division, then that is where you'll go. And if that is where you go, then it is far too easy to take oxygen from others along the way. If what gets your focus is connection, vision, purpose, and solutions, then that is where you'll go.

This book will focus on six mindsets, behaviors, and actions that I have personally observed, experienced, studied, and practiced within teams and organizations. In a world that is often noisy, negative, gossipy, and critical, our mindset is vital. The individuals and teams who harness mindsets and action that breathe life into themselves and those on the journey with them will navigate the road with more grace and effectiveness than those who don't.

These aren't the only mindsets and actions needed by leaders in the world today, but these six mindsets and actions are undoubtedly needed for the road ahead. If we can shift our eyes and our hearts and practice inhaling this oxygen into ourselves and then providing energy to our teammates, progress will be made. Let's breathe with mindsets that fuel clarity, inclusivity, agility, grit, rest, and ownership.

Disclaimer: Nothing about changing your mindset or the culture of a group of people is easy. Quick solutions do not exist. What you are about to read might seem simple, but it is achievable only with dedicated leadership, practice, commitment, and persistence. For the overly analytical person reading this book, please recognize the breathing analogy is not meant to be literal but is rather a metaphor to expand our awareness and learning. I recognize there are many nuances to the ways our bodies operate and utilize oxygen. This is not a scientific book; it's a metaphor to stimulate thinking. Thank you for reading it with that spirit.

Warning: Courageously committing to breathing the oxygen of the mindsets and actions laid out in this book actually will change the culture of your relationships and teams. Your internal environment and your external environments will change. Enter at your own risk.

Choose to breathe in good air.

"It's a lack of clarity that creates chaos and frustration. Those emotions are poison to any living goal."

—Steve Maraboli

CHAPTER 2

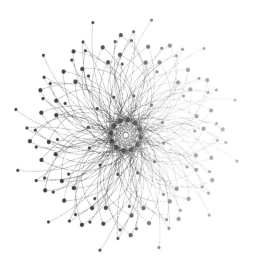

CLARITY
Vision + Direction

Our minds crave clarity of vision and direction. The best leaders breathe oxygen into themselves and their team by improving everyone's sight lines.

About twenty years ago, you probably had never heard of Gonzaga University. If you had heard of it, chances are you didn't know it was in Spokane, Washington, and were not able to locate it on a map. That was just twenty years ago.

For basketball fans, it is hard to imagine the landscape of college basketball without Gonzaga, but that is why their story is so compelling and reaches far beyond sports. The meteoric rise of Gonzaga basketball is a story of vision plus leadership plus culture and is relevant for every team, organization, or entity on the planet.

In the early '90s, Gonzaga University was not in good financial standing. Enrollment was down, and the university and brand were limping along. They had just brought in their smallest freshmen class—five hundred students—and the athletic program was hemorrhaging money by all accounts. That's when athletic director Mike Roth had the gall and vision to suggest that the way forward was to actually invest more money into the men's basketball program. Surprisingly, university president Father Robert Spitzer agreed.

In that moment, the vision began to take shape. They dreamed that the notoriety of the basketball program on a national landscape could shine a positive light on the wonderful educational opportunities happening at the school and on the charming but relatively unknown city of Spokane. They had watched how a university like Georgetown had risen to national prominence in the 1980s and helped provide tremendous financial support to the university mission. They immediately began investing in their program, rebranding their logo and image, and investing in local television deals to begin the journey.

In 1999, just a few years after the initial reinvestment back into the program, Gonzaga experienced a magical run to the Elite Eight in the March Madness national championship tournament. Gonzaga was on the map for the first time, and the courageous vision was in motion. But many small schools have had one Cinderella run in the tournament only to disappear back into nothingness for years. Gonzaga's consistency in leadership and in strategic and intentional development of the culture is worthy of its own entire book.

The vision had clarity and direction. That doesn't mean it was easy, or else everyone would have done it, and Gonzaga wouldn't be this amazing example. They had clarity on how the mission of the basketball program connected with the overall university mission. They had clarity on the type of leadership they wanted and needed for the journey. Assistant coach Mark Few was promoted to head coach following the 1999 run. He began to build a family culture, where every person associated with the program was "pulling the rope in the same direction."

They had clarity on the types of players they needed to recruit and the style of play they needed in order to compete. Because they were a "midmajor" in those days, they knew they couldn't compete in the recruiting wars for the top talents with the traditional powers in college basketball. Instead, they took a different strategy than most schools and, ahead of their time, began investing in the scouting of international players. They had clarity of vision, clarity of direction, and clarity of leadership toward their culture, skill set, and style of play.

What has followed over the last twenty years is nothing short of remarkable. It's why the story is relevant to any team or entity. Gonzaga has now made the NCAA tournament twenty-two straight years. (The only schools with longer streaks are Kansas, Duke, and Michigan State.) They've made it to six consecutive Sweet Sixteens, the nation's longest active streak. They've reached the Elite Eight four of the last six years. (No other team can say the same.) They have won more tournament games in the last five years than anyone, have the current longest active streaks of any school ranked in the top twenty-five (at ninety-plus consecutive weeks), and was the consensus number one team in the country for twenty consecutive weeks to end the 2020-21 season. They have now played in two national championship games in the last five years, and it appears that it is only a matter of time before they cut down the nets. They entered the 2021–22 season as the preseason number one team again.

Those metrics and their performance are now undeniable. How they got here is even more impressive. The basketball metrics are an unbelievable story in of itself, as are the rosters over the years, which have overflowed with talented players from Russia, Japan, Serbia, France, Africa, and many other spots around the globe. The vision and execution of the plan to find talent, develop talent, and assimilate the talent into a culture and system when a language barrier also often exists is incredible. Their on-court analytics have also been mesmerizing, leading the country in offensive efficiency for three straight years. They are like poetry to watch.

fense continues to improve, and now they are legitimate contenders, year in and year out. They are able to recruit the biggest names, and the culture they have built has become their competitive advantage.

The off-court metrics for the overall university mission over the last twenty years are quite impressive too. Since 1999, the university's enrollment has doubled to more than 7,500 students, and admissions applications have tripled. The school's annual budget has risen from $72.7 million in 1999 to $283 million in 2017. The university's rise over the last twenty years is tied to its basketball program.

Every year, Coach Mark Few gathers with the university president, the athletic director, and other key leaders to make sure they are still aligned on the vision and direction of the program. They make sure they are still "pulling the rope in the same direction."

They are an example for all to be inspired by. It can happen. It is possible. Vision, leadership, and culture matter.

 ## CLEAR IS KIND. UNCLEAR IS UNKIND.

Some of the most important oxygen we breathe as leaders and share with others is about clarity. Clarity of mission, vision, and values is critical, as is clarity of expectations and roles.

Being kind is a great thing. I'm all for it. But I've come to know and appreciate that being kind isn't just about being "nice." We should all be nice, don't be confused, but a broader definition of kindness might also benefit us all.

Author and researcher Brené Brown reminds us in her book *Dare to Lead* that clear is kind and unclear is unkind. I love that language. Her book is about the daring style of leadership that is needed to have courageous conversations with those that we are on the journey with. Giving honest feedback is kind. Talking smack about someone behind their back is unkind. Healthy leaders and teams become very good at wading into uncomfortable discussions in pursuit of clarity on expectations, observations, and support. As I say to many of my clients, *conversations are the currency for change.* If we want anything to change, then we had better be ready to talk about it.

In a world where chaos, frustration, and noise are rampant, clarity is kind. Helping people find clarity in the midst of experiencing thin air is kind and necessary. It helps them breathe easier. People crave direction. They want meaning. They want to know *why* you're going on the journey and what you're trying to accomplish (mission). They want to know *where* you're heading and what future you're aiming for (vision). They want to know how you're committed to travel together as a team and what will be your compass for the journey (values). They want to know *what* the game plan is for the next actions and *who* has ownership for what (strategy).

Gonzaga was (and appears to be at this point) aligned at the macro level of the president, athletic department, board of regents, and head coach on the mission, vision, values, and strategy for the road ahead. Every year they must make time to gain clarity and return to alignment on all those key principles. It's the foundation for the temperature they desire to set daily.

As I talk about in my book *Thermostat Cultures*, the best team cultures know the temperature they are trying to set in everything they do and proactively shape the culture they want. Some leaders and teams operate in thermometer mode, in which they are purely reactionary and do not know the temperature they are trying to set. The best are proactive, intentional, and purposeful in setting the temperature for their culture. Thermostat Cultures are dynamic and committed to calibrating their thermostats. Gonzaga is also aligned at the micro level as players, assistant coaches, trainers, and all staff throughout the athletic department as they carry out those principles. They are committed to clarity with each other on the mission, vision, values, and strategy for the day-to-day operations. It's the temperature they set daily by the way they speak, act, interact, train, and collaborate.

Teams and entire organizations are sometimes aligned at the

ı those principles but not at the micro level. And ey are aligned at the micro level but not the macro re needed.

ne a leader is able to breathe oxygen into the people aroun n with clarity on vision and direction, it gives a boost of energy, purpose, and alignment on the metaphorical rope they are all pulling in unison. Every time a leader is unable to articulate clarity on the vision and direction, then oxygen is starved from the team and the culture feels scattered, chaotic, and confusing. Energy is sapped, and therefore people hesitate. It's hard to breathe.

When truth and direction become cloudy, direct communication is needed. Oxygen that provides clarity is kind and necessary.

THE SOCIAL DILEMMA

It's hard to know what is true anymore. Things aren't always clear. In fact, most things around us are quite blurry. In the documentary *The Social Dilemma*, creators, coders, and design engineers from Google, Facebook, Pinterest, Instagram, Twitter, and other social platforms share their knowledge and observations about the social media world. They provide insights on the creation of the tools within the technology that seek to engage, manipulate, and profit off our interests.

The documentary dives into the psychology behind why some of the "like" buttons and other features were created in order to drive engagement, addiction, and screen time. It not only points out the studies about the decline of people's mental health and the correlation with higher volumes of social media activity, but it centers on the manipulation of the tools around the general question of what is true.

We've all witnessed this in our own lives and gathering of information. The term "fake news" has become so commonplace due to the ways a myriad of groups are using the social tools to perpetuate misinformation, division, and anxiety by utilizing the algorithms to deliver stories that reinforce someone's viewpoint. The creators of these tools are sounding the alarm that the tools themselves have gotten out of hand and the profit of a person's attention is more valuable that delivering truth. The case the documentary makes is that we are being divided by these tools and fed information that is blurring the truth for all.

I'm not sharing this to scare your pants off or to run screaming that social media is 100 percent bad. I'm grateful for the amazing ways we've been able to connect and share with friends around the globe, to share positive vibes with those having babies, getting married, celebrating a birthday, a new job, or messages of support to those recovering from surgery. I'm grateful that organ donors have been connected and support groups formed. But I'm also aware that misinformation is rampant and is making clarity very illusive at times.

In a noisy world where media and algorithms are often divisive by design, feeding us stories to manipulate our thoughts, our ability to seek clarity with others and breathe oxygen into ourselves and others is as important as ever. When our newsfeed doesn't provide objective content, or the person on the other side of the table is being fed the exact opposite narrative on an issue or event, communication plus vision plus direction is critical. When we're bombarded by rumors, conspiracies, and gossip that profit from creating division rather than connection, then we must seek it out directly. We must create connection, sit face-to-face, and reconnect to our collective vision and direction. It calls for a spirit of leadership that seeks to provide clarity, kindness, and connection and to breathe life into a culture that wants to listen and collaborate. We have the opportunity to claim our own attention and choose to look in the same direction, together.

TRIANGULATION

This phenomenon happens in every group dynamic on the planet. You know how it goes. A triangle has three points of view: Person A, Person B, and Person C. Person A has a problem, disagreement, misunderstanding, or conflict with Person B. But who does Person A go find? You got it, Person C. Hence, triangulation occurs.

Person A seeks out Person C, and it typically goes something like this (cue the *Saturday Night Live* teenage Valley Girl voice): "Can you believe what Person B did?" the rant begins. "They said this and did that," the rant continues. Things escalate quickly. Soon Person A is worked up and this incident is now a reflection of the whole team, and the entire organization is sinking.

I hope you're laughing or at least giggling at this point. You probably are, because you know this dynamic happens in every group of human beings. Because we're all human and imperfect, chances are we've all played each of these three roles at some time or another. Triangulation is happening in every team culture. It just depends on whether it's a culture that is breathing oxygen into each other or one that is not.

You see, Person C plays an enormous role in the health of every team culture. Because they typically can take one of two paths when Person A comes looking for them. They can either take the easy path, which I refer to as "breathing oxygen into the flames," or the harder but kinder and healthier path in a Thermostat Culture of "breathing oxygen into the people."

"Breathing oxygen into the flames" means that Person B focuses on the fire rather than on the person. Breathing oxygen into the flames is negative gossip. They add fuel to the fire by responding with, "They said what? I can't believe them." Their gasping response begins. "You're right, they are awful." Momentum is building. "This place is going up in flames!" And the flames are now a bonfire.

We rationalize this response on both sides by saying we're just "venting." In some ways, it just feels good that a team member or friend chose us to confide in. Selfishly, it feels good to be Person C. It's easy to fan the flames and then walk away. The problem is when that happens, the brush fire isn't contained, and it doesn't go away. Now three (or more) people are involved, and the issue hasn't been resolved. The fire festers.

In healthy, committed teams that are Thermostat Cultures and clear on their mission, vision, values, and strategy, Person C takes the other path of breathing oxygen into the people. Instead of the focus being on the fire, the focus is on the two human beings involved. A thermostat reads the temperature in the room and then adjusts to set the desired temperature. Person C listens, absorbs, and seeks to understand. They ask clarifying questions to try to understand the situation without passing judgment. Then, when the time is right and Person A has communicated what they needed to share, Person C is able to breathe oxygen into the people.

"I'm sorry you're frustrated and upset," they begin in some form or fashion to help validate Person A that we're all human and conflict happens. "But I know Person B, and I doubt they really feel that way. Something must have gotten lost in translation, or you're both missing each other's point of view," C continues. "It sounds like you and Person B need to sit down directly and discuss this so you can get on the same page. As your friend and team member, I'll check back with you in a week to see how that conversation went." Person C breathes oxygen with clarity back into the situation to encourage the two people to connect. Taking a step back and deep breaths are needed. Breathing oxygen into the person allows room for vulnerability and encourages solutions. It's not about the gossip, it's about the positive path forward.

I often ask teams if this is realistic. Some eye rolls and "this will never work" looks ensue. And then, usually, a lively dialogue concludes that it is in fact realistic, just difficult. It's easier to take the other path and breathe oxygen into the flames rather than the person. But clarity is kind. And teams and organizations that have a culture with clear values for *how* they are committed to working together tend to get better with having *conversations that are the currency for change* and getting everyone back pulling in the same direction.

Amazing progress, morale, and connection are possible in team cultures where the leaders actively practice breathing oxygen into the people rather than into the flames. In team cultures where opposite is true, toxicity, division, and poison spread throughout the group. These team cultures become siloed, and people's own personal interests are the agenda. It takes oxygen from the room. It makes it hard for anyone to breathe.

TWO-WAY STREET

It is easier for relationships and teams to find clarity when there is a foundation of clarity on the mission (why), vision (where), values (how), and strategy (what and who) from the beginning. As I say in *Thermostat Cultures*, language drives behavior. Clearly articulated language linked to desired actions and behaviors creates a compass for the journey.

Still, every relationship and every single team anchor the language each time they return to dialogue about the compass together. If they have nurtured a culture that isn't a "top-down" style of leadership and exhibits the "upside-down pyramid" approach, then each person sees their encounters as a two-way street. No conversations are one-way streets; they are collaborative, where each participant plays an active role. Again, this doesn't mean that two people might not have different roles and different seniority in the organizational design, but they both honor the perspective of the other and recognize both parties play a role in future progress.

With the teams and organizations I consult and partner with to help strengthen their development of leaders, culture, and clarity of mission, vision, and values, healthy communications are essential. We talk and develop foundational elements of having effective one-on-one conversations and team huddles. Every good conversation (even the uncomfortable, courageous ones) begins with taking a deep breath and entering the room with the human element in mind—honoring the human being on the other side of the table. Choosing to enter the room with the spirit that you want things to progress, you show you want the best for the person and acknowledge in your mind that it is a two-way-street relationship. Every effective conversation acknowledges the things that are going well and the specifics that both parties are doing that are in alignment with your cultural values. Then it is also about being honest and clear (kind) about the areas that fall short of the standards we've identified together for the culture of our team or relationship. The conversation is two-way, and both parties share their point of view. It doesn't mean that we shy away from honesty and firm development, but we're committed to progress together. Every effective one-on-one or team huddle ends with clarifying what the next actions are to "set a new temperature" and determine who is doing what. A mutual timeline is established to touch base again so that both participants understand and buy into the commitment to progress, together. Two-way street.

My wife, Amy, and I have committed to a yearly "visioning retreat" for some years now. We carve out two days in our schedules to get out of our house to connect and have two-way conversations that are the currency for change. The structure of our time shifts a tiny bit each year, depending on what we may have to discuss, but the general format stays the same. We spend most of the first day looking through the rearview mirror of the past year. We acknowledge celebrations in our lives (personal, professional, spiritual, family growth, friends, marriage, and finances) and also acknowledge the obstacles that were challenges.

Day two is focused on shifting our eyes to the windshield for the year ahead and identifying goals or intentions we have in each of those areas. It is a robust dialogue centered around the question, "What is the life we want to cocreate together, and who do we hope to be in the world?" Each time we share together in this way, we are anchoring the language and values we've always discussed about the type of marriage, family, and life we are hoping to lead. We have fun, eat well, and celebrate life together. It's a two-way street.

TRUST THE PROCESS

You've heard the phrase thousands of times: "Trust the process."

Coaches, CEOs, department heads, educators, and political leaders have said it for years.

process.

...se is uttered typically when a leader is attempting to

...to his team in the midst of uncertainty, ambiguity,

...rocky times. But why is it so difficult for people to truly trust the process?

There are four main reasons people struggle with a leader who repeatedly says, "Trust the process."

First, it all has to do with that first word, trust. Most strong relationships, teams, and partnerships begin and end with that word. Human beings may make a choice to trust someone (and I do believe it begins with a choice), but the reality is that trust isn't just blindly given and received by people. Trust is currency that is bartered moment by moment every single day. Every relationship and interaction with people is either building social equity and trust with them or is chipping away at and deteriorating that trust. Each day, the equity in that relationship goes up and down. The healthiest and most stable relationships are able to enter more challenging conversations and experiences because they have built up enough social equity and trust over time.

Second, and related to that daily bartering of trust, we don't just blindly trust the process because many times the leader or messenger who is pleading with us to trust has not built up enough social equity as a leader. In situations where teams hesitate, it's a symptom of a lack of trust. Their words in the past might not have always been backed up with action. It's difficult to trust the process when the messenger hasn't always proven to follow through and elicit the kind of trust they are requesting.

Third, and perhaps as significant as anything else, it's difficult to trust the process when team members aren't clear on what the actual process is. It's easy to ask for trust, but it's harder to actually articulate a clear path forward. When teams hesitate to trust the process, then it oftentimes is connected to a lack of clarity around the path they see out the windshield: *why* they're going (mission), *where* they're heading (vision), *how* they're committed to travel (values), and *what* steps they are going to take to stimulate progress (strategy). Lack of clarity on these foundational elements makes everything out the windshield seem blurry.

Finally, trusting the process isn't always easy, because it takes time. The process usually doesn't provide immediate gratification, and many people find it difficult to be patient because of their desire for instant results. People want the good stuff right away and want things to happen quickly and easily. Unfortunately, developing people, culture, and a vision that is worth chasing isn't a drive-through experience. It doesn't happen overnight, and so it requires teams to stay focused, patient, disciplined—delaying that need for instant gratification. Working the process takes leaders and teams who are committed and adept at keeping everyone looking in the same direction.

That's what builds trust. One action after another over time.

Every time we breathe oxygen into the people around us that brings clarity to the path forward, it gives energy and life to the room. It clears up the windshield and breathes life into people for the next stretch of the road to travel.

Clarity is kind and essential. We need it in the air we breathe.

**Are your
WHY (mission),
WHERE (vision),
HOW (values), and
WHAT (strategy)
clear?**

BREATHING OXYGEN

If clear is kind, are the mission (why), vision (where), values (how), and strategy (what) clear and connected to the actions and behaviors you want to perpetuate within your team and relationships? Are expectations clear and practiced?

INHALE

- Establish clear language for the mission, vision, values, and strategy.
- Describe roles, and express clear expectations.
- Make time to connect as a team and to build key relationships to align clarity.
- Inhale gratitude, celebrations, and appreciation.

EXHALE

- Scattered, confusing, and blurry communication.
- Blame, gossip, excuses, and wasted energy.
- Doubt, worry, and items out of your control.

Notes

"When we listen and celebrate what is both common and different, we become wiser, more inclusive, and better organizations."

—Pat Wadors

CHAPTER 3

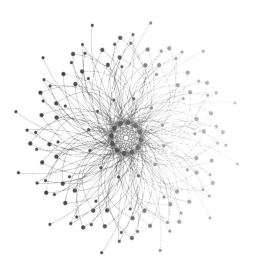

INCLUSIVITY
Participatory + Alignment

Every time the circle is widened to include and welcome people to the table to bring their gifts to the mission, oxygen fills the room.

It was field day at my daughter's elementary school, and I was one of the parent volunteers. I was sent to the tug-of-war station. A loud siren went off every fifteen minutes to signal each class to rotate to the next station, and a new batch of kids would come racing and screaming to my station.

If you haven't played tug-of-war in a while, then you may forget that it generally loses its luster after about one or two contests. But I always had fifteen minutes to kill! So, creativity was king. I had to come up with something to stall for time and keep the kids interested and having fun. Then, *aha*! A "can't lose" idea occurred.

"Who wants to play boys versus girls?"

Mayhem would erupt every time. The classic gender battle was the perfect thing to awaken their souls and dig even deeper into their competitive wells. Every single time I would announce this question, the same thing would happen, in class after class, all morning long. The elementary school kids who identify as boys would immediately begin flexing their muscles, chest bumping, talking trash, and giggling as if this was going to be their moment to show their pure dominance over the girls. The excitement and tension were palpable.

As the boys were hooting and hollering with each other, I would slowly make my way over to the girls' side of the rope. Perhaps I was biased because I was there for my daughter (although I have two wonderful boys too). The girls were quiet and would actually look at me and listen to the advice I was giving. In a quiet voice, I would give the girls a couple of tips.

"Align your team on the rope in zipper fashion, one on one side of the rope and one on the other, all the way down the rope," I would begin. "Pick a captain, and when the contest begins, the captain yells out, 'One, two, three,' and everyone pulls together on three. Got it?"

The girls would nod their heads and instantly go into organizational mode. Sure enough, the boys were still over there giggling, jumping up and down, and showing off their underdeveloped biceps.

I would take my position on the center of the rope and say the famous, "On your marks, get set, *go!*" Each time my cadence reached the crescendo of "*go,*" the boys were still running in and scrambling for their place on the rope. Each would grab the rope wherever they were and start tugging on it with all their might. The problem was, since there was zero organization and coordination, all their little muscles were pulling in slightly different directions and actually creating more friction on the rope. In many ways, they were pulling against each other.

Meanwhile, the kids who identify as girls would be nicely

organized on the rope. The captain would yell out, "One, two, three," and like a well-oiled machine, the girls would all pull in unison. It would typically take about three pulls before the girls had quickly dominated the boys.

Mayhem would ensue. An upheaval would call for a "redo." We'd line it up again, and the same result would take place.

It's now abundantly clear what Gonzaga's Mark Few meant when he talked about "all people pulling the rope in the same direction." Because it doesn't just magically happen. It takes co-ordination, organization, and clarity on how and what direction we're going and how we are committed to pulling the rope, and it must be inclusive of everyone. All the people play a role. Not just the biggest. Not just the strongest. Not just those in key positions or privileged roles. All means all. The tug-of-war contest is most effective when *all* are included and clear on how we're committed to pulling the rope. We're stronger together.

With all the recent talk about the future of work, it has become clear that leaders and employers have a tremendous opportunity to lead the way in creating inclusive environments. World events in the last several years have made it abundantly clear that there is much progress to be made in terms of including and welcoming diversity of backgrounds, thought, and experience to the table. Progress is made by leaning into courageous conversations around bias and systematic power and will require leaders who are seeking equity and justice for all people. The most compelling leaders and organizations on the planet won't be perfect, but they will breathe oxygen into cultures that seek progress in all these areas. Widening the circle and creating more inclusive teams breathe life and energy into the culture.

GEORGE FLOYD

After the brutal, inhumane, and horrifying video of George Floyd's death on the streets of Minneapolis, national outrage and dialogue pushed through the surface. Right in front of our eyes, a human being's oxygen was literally taken from him. Unfortunately, this wasn't the first act of this kind, and it wouldn't be the last. But this one brought people to the streets and raised the conversation to the national level in a way I had not seen or experienced in my life.

The Black Lives Matter movement and dialogue about systemic racism and the power and need for diversity, equity, and inclusion were top of mind for all. As a white male, I knew my first role was to listen. And so I took that role and posture seriously and reached out in support to those in my network and to my friends. I sent emails of support, invited guests to my podcast, and hosted my own virtual event (Thermostat Cultures Live) to share, listen, and have conversations that are the currency for change. Friends and guests like Kendall Harrell, chief people officer at Caribou Coffee; Kevin Clayton, VP of diversity, inclusion, and engagement for the Cleveland Cavaliers; and Lachandra Baker, senior manager for employee engagement at CoverMyMeds, jumped into the conversation. So did Howard Behar, former president of Starbucks Coffee; Doug Ulman, CEO of Pelotonia; Ken Bouyer, Ernst & Young Americas' inclusiveness recruiting leader; Lori Turner, VP of leadership for Educational Equity; and former NBA number one draft pick Greg Oden. It was a powerful collection of voices, hearts, and wisdom.

In all of those challenging and hopeful conversations, one thing was abundantly clear: there is more work to be done by all. I was as much a student as anyone. But I also needed to share my voice and ideas so that *all* were contributing to the dialogue. Leaders of all backgrounds have the opportunity and necessity to create more inclusive environments. In the next decade (and beyond), perhaps the greatest action leaders will take is to widen their team circles to be more inclusive and invest time and resources more purposefully to align *all* on the rope. Leaders who breathe oxygen of inclusivity and a mindset that we are stronger together into their own life and those around them will be more compelling, influential, and effective in all they do. We must be proactive in our efforts to engage.

I truly believe that our places of work are going to play a

tremendous role in leading the change. Employers (leaders) and the people within their ecosystems will be the ones to help create environments where people are welcomed, educated, cared for, and able to have courageous conversations about topics that challenge us. Leaders within organizations will be the ones who help us practice working with people and backgrounds who are different than us. Leaders who are able to breathe oxygen into teams that help people come together and navigate their way through life while being connected to a powerful organizational mission will breathe oxygen that stimulates progress.

SKEPTICISM VERSUS CYNICISM

In order for progress to be made, the nature of our conversations together must improve.

My friend Doug Ulman is the CEO of Pelotonia, the inspiring organization supporting cancer research. He once shared a story about former CBS evening news anchor Dan Rather that I continue to ponder. On his way back from a business trip, Doug was on the airplane as the final passengers were boarding. They were only moments away from the plane pulling out onto the runway when one of the final passengers made his way down the aisle—Dan Rather.

Of the few empty seats still remaining on the airplane, to Doug's surprise, Dan sat down in the empty seat next to him. Doug's first impression was that Dan was a very nice man who seemed happy to chat. The two of them began small talk, even though Doug was cognizant of not pushing the conversation, in case Dan didn't want to be bothered. The chatting continued.

Doug had already had his laptop open and had been typing away, and so Dan just assumed he was working and talking at the same time. Doug was so impressed by the conversation and didn't want to forget the details that he actually quit working and just started typing notes of their encounter while they spoke. He was glad he did.

As the conversation ebbed and flowed across the culture in America and the way things have changed over the years, Dan made an interesting observation.

"You know, when we were being trained as journalists, we were taught to be skeptical," Rather began. "We were taught to ask clarifying and skeptical questions that would help better understand the position of the person we were interviewing or story we were covering. It was critical to ask questions that helped others understand why someone thought a particular way or why the story was playing out the way it was. Skepticism was a valuable tool to better understand.

"Nowadays, though, it seems like nobody is interested in asking skeptical questions to better understand someone's point of view," he continued. "Rather, everything seems to be cynical. And the difference between skepticism and cynicism is a big difference. Instead of asking questions to better understand, everyone is asking leading questions to try to 'get' the other person. Questions to lead the story or create a cynical narrative."

This distinction between skepticism and cynicism has been a very important thought for me in the last year. In a world that does seem to be leaning more cynical (just watch the news or peek at social media), are we as leaders asking questions to better understand people and situations, or are we perpetuating cynical narratives?

The inclusive leader who breathes oxygen into themselves and those around them is someone who is able to ask skeptical questions with the intent of better understanding someone's point of view or the situation they are facing. Intent and spirit are everything. Leaders who lead with an intention and spirit of understanding will breathe oxygen into those around them. Leaders who lead with a cynical mindset always trying to "get" the other person or lead a false narrative will take oxygen from the room.

If we aim to be more inclusive and align *all* on the rope to pull in the same direction, then our intent and spirit must reflect that of understanding rather than catching the other person. Give oxygen, don't take oxygen.

STICKERS, NOT TATTOOS

Even in our desire to be inclusive, diverse, and equitable toward all around us, every human makes mistakes. There have been countless examples of well-intended leaders or members of teams who have misspoken, used hurtful language, or made ignorant comments. This has happened and will continue to happen. None of us is perfect. I'm not making excuses, I'm just urging us all to leave some room for grace. The exact diversity of background, thought, and experience that will make us stronger also creates an environment where people have different experiences and unconscious biases. In the process of discovering them, becoming more aware, and widening the circle for all, we'll need grace with each other.

I remember a conversation I was a part of with Dr. Melissa Crum, an equity and diversity practitioner, where she shared a powerful image. She spoke eloquently as she shared specific examples where team members had been labeled harsh terms like "racist," "sexist," or "homophobic" after making ignorant comments. She was clear that the person's comments were not intentional and calculated with the intent to harm or damage someone, just uninformed. She expressed the need for more empathy and grace within these conversations when it is clear no harm was intentional. The image she shared was that we need our labels with people to be "stickers, not tattoos."

Stickers are temporary and an opportunity to learn and then remove. Tattoos are permanent. They scar. They stay with someone forever. Many comments by members of our teams that are not intended to be hurtful don't need to be tattoos. They might be better thought of as stickers. The people who made them might need empathy. They might need grace. Leaders help bring oxygen into these situations.

EVERY THOUGHT, WORD, AND ACTION VIBRATES

In *Thermostat Cultures,* I speak about how culture is dynamic. This is an important distinction because many leaders, teams, and companies get tricked into thinking that culture is a static place that you arrive at once you're able to name the culture you want. Then they can declare that they've "focused on culture" and can now move on to the next initiative because the culture is now "set."

The reality is that culture is always changing. Whenever a leader, team, or company says to me, "We want to change our culture," I politely reply, "Good, because it is already changing." Culture is dynamic; it changes every moment. The question isn't, "Is your culture changing?" It is. The more compelling question is, "What role are we going to play in what the culture becomes?" You must intentionally impact the ecosystem of your culture to proactively lead in the direction you desire.

The ecosystem of a culture changes moment by moment by the way that everyone in the ecosystem thinks, acts, and interacts. Each contribution of thought, action, and interaction contributes (or does damage) to the culture. Everything shared throughout the ecosystem matters. Each thought, word, action, interaction, meeting, process, policy, brand message, office design, and compensation and benefits package matters. It all cocreates the culture one moment at a time, one breath at a time. Leaders who breathe oxygen into their culture are proactive about the thinking, acting, and interacting that contribute to their cultural ecosystem. The most compelling leaders on Earth in the future will be the ones who become more inclusive in their vision, approach, and actions. The vision won't just serve a select few or an exclusive group but will be about creating and expanding a more inclusive ecosystem of thinking, acting, and interacting.

We all have a presence when we come into a room, and that presence sends vibrations to those around us. We can't control everything about what people feel about us, but we can become more mindful about how we enter and what is the focal point of our vibrations.

Vibrations are felt when a boss rushes hurriedly into her office while on a phone call and doesn't make eye contact with the staff members along her path. Vibrations are felt when the CEO or department head uses language that excludes rather than includes. Vibrations are felt when a spouse tunes out their partner during a dinner conversation or shuns a gesture of personal touch and intimacy. Vibrations are felt when a coach looks deeply into a player's eyes and says, "I believe in you." Vibrations are felt when a teacher expresses care and empathy for a student who is experiencing struggles at home.

In her enlightening book *Contagious Culture*, Anese Cavanaugh refers to this as vibrational energy. Moment by moment each day our presence is sending energy (good and sometimes bad) to those around us. She encourages all of us to ask ourselves these three questions as we enter situations:

- *Is my presence hurting or helping the impact I want to have?*
- *Is my presence adding to or detracting from the quality of the energy in the room?*
- *Will my presence make others—and myself—feel better or worse?*

If we know that our spirit and vibrations are contagious, then what are you spreading? Are your vibrations inclusive, and do they invite all to have a place on the rope your team is pulling in your metaphorical tug-of-war? Are your vibrations aligned with the mission of your team and bringing out the best in those around you? Is your vibe enhancing the culture or detracting from it? Is your vibe breathing oxygen into the room or taking oxygen from the room? Aligning with other people begins with our willingness to take ownership for the presence we bring to the relationship and the energy we contribute. How we feel and the oxygen we share with those around us create powerful momentum that is often hard to explain or identify. Our vibrations and the oxygen we breathe and share with others impact the energy in the room.

CROSS-ORGANIZATIONAL RELATIONSHIPS

Earlier in the book, I referenced Wesley Adams and Tamara Myles's research on "The Ten Principles of Highly Meaningful Work," based on data collected from the exemplar organizations they studied. All ten principles are important (but not shocking), and their study is affirming in so many ways to the tenets of culture-shaping and leadership development I speak and consult about.

Two of the critical principles that jump out from their research that are in direct alignment with leaders who breathe oxygen of inclusivity into their teams are the principles to "foster cross-organizational relationships" and "engage and embrace the whole person."

Exemplar organizations and cultures intentionally create environments that foster strong relationships and a sense of belonging. Their employees report a feeling that their leaders and all within the organization strive to make them feel like they are part of a healthy family. They feel their leaders initiate supportive cultures that build collective identity and encourage care and connection. The titans of industry that everyone always points to, as well as the smaller exemplar organizations you may have never heard of, understand the power of diverse, inclusive, and cross-organizational relationships beyond just your immediate team. Collective identity, care, and connection are embraced and intentional across teams, departments, and differences.

These exemplar organizations also strive to create conditions that enable employees to bring their whole selves to work. They want people to embrace their uniqueness, share and celebrate differences, and encourage individuals to engage authentically. Part of the air they breathe is seeking to understand the uniqueness of others and helping individuals live and work authentically as part of a collective whole.

All of these examples and validated research point out the intentionality of culture-shaping. Throughout each leader, each team, each department, and across the entire organization, specific oxygen mindsets and actions are inhaled, and others are exhaled.

The air they choose to breathe and how they fuel their mind and actions are everything. The best leaders are focused more on the *eco* rather than the *ego*. Their focus is on the cultural ecosystem they are nurturing, watering, and pruning. Their daily pursuits are aimed at giving oxygen to the plants in the ecosystem rather than hoarding all the oxygen for their own needs (ego).

PARTICIPATORY

We live in a participatory world. We have for some time now. As we breathe oxygen into the cultures within our teams and organizations, we must be aware of how the people who make up our teams are moving throughout the world.

Stop for a second and think about what is popular in the world today. What are the popular restaurants, experiences, and trends? How are most people moving through the world today? Consider the fact that we now live in a participatory world. Let me share some profound examples.

Years ago, it was Starbucks that taught us we didn't just want a cup of coffee, we wanted to share in the creation of our own cup of coffee. Howard Behar, the former president of Starbucks, is a great friend and has been a wonderful mentor to me. His stories about Starbucks taking off are a fascinating study in connecting with people. Starbucks didn't want you to just order a coffee. They wanted you to participate in the process of making your unique cup of coffee. So you and billions of others now have walked into a Starbucks to tell the barista that you would like a double this with extra that. They were clear they were in the people business serving coffee, not the other way around.

Think about Chipotle, the chain that practically created the new "fast casual" restaurant market. When you walk into a Chipotle, you participate in the creation of your own meal. You walk down the line and pick your unique combination of the items they have to design your special meal. You don't just order a burrito; you actively choose what you would like to put into your unique burrito. Did you know that the fast casual restaurant market in the last decade has reached more than $21 billion in size? Evidently, we like the cost, the freshness, and, I would add, our ability to participate in the process.

Another example is fantasy football, which *Forbes* estimates to be a $70 billion market (and growing). I'm in a loyal and committed (and the best in the world) fantasy football league, and I can tell you that we are not alone in our fascination with picking the players and competing with those around us. We don't want to just watch the game; we want to participate in the experience.

Video games are predominately all experiential. You don't just play a video game, you immerse yourself with friends and strangers into an experience that you all are having together. The game *Fortnite* became a worldwide phenomenon and has amassed over 350 million players around the world participating in the experience. And other games have followed.

And, of course, social media is the greatest example of today's participatory world. According to a 2021 study, there are an estimated 3.96 billion active social media users in the world, with a high percentage of people spending two to three hours daily interacting on social networks. The social media growth rate has been increasing globally at about 12 percent year over year since 2015. We want to share things, tell what we like, comment, and be part of the discussion. We are a participatory culture.

This is extremely important to remember as you begin to engage with the people in your teams and organizations. They don't want things handed down from above. They don't want a memo or email with news about their job. They want to participate.

This is the time we live in, and I would argue that we always have wanted to participate. The best leaders breathe oxygen into their people by including them so they have a voice, feel valued, and get to participate in the creation of your culture. Leaders actively include others in the visioning, dreaming, and aspiring for their future.

Why is this important beyond your team members desiring a voice in your visioning process? Your people, or the other members on your team, cannot possibly see what's going on in your head. Everyone on the team lives only within their own heads. It takes work to align the group and get them sharing in the vision they want to design.

This does not mean that everything on your team or in your company needs to be by consensus or discussed by all, but these trends do reveal to us that your people want to participate. They don't want everything dictated from above or delivered in a cookie-cutter sound bite. Where appropriate, they want to have a voice, a buy-in, ownership in the direction you're heading. They want to participate in the creation of the culture.

Generationally speaking, Millennials (those aged twenty-five to forty in 2022) are now the largest generation in the American workforce, and they want to participate. They want to be aligned with each other and with the direction you're heading.

One who aims at nothing hits it every time. If you do not have clarity about the culture you desire or what your people would like to create, then anything goes. If you aren't intentional about the mindsets and oxygen you are breathing into yourself as a leader and the teams around you, then anything goes. Remember, the culture is changing already. It's changing as we speak. It is dynamic. It will continue to change. The question is, will you actively participate in the creation of what you want it to become?

BETTER TOGETHER

Back to tug-of-war. Intellectually, we know that we can't pull the rope alone. We know we alone can't accomplish a mission that is greater than ourselves. We know that we alone can't bring the entire vision to life. We need partners. We need support. We need teammates. We need others.

We're stronger together. Participatory plus alignment.

Intellectually, we know that too. But the eighteen-inch journey from our cognitive mind to our heart that compels action is longer than we often imagine. We get tricked into trying to do things alone.

We pull the rope as hard as we can, but not in alignment with others. In many ways, it's easier that way. It's easier to just grab the rope and pull it as hard as we can. But we know that's not most effective.

Twenty-first century leaders increasingly understand that their role is to get the right people on the rope. It's their role to expand the reach and include more people on the rope. Their role is to align people and their gifts and strengths to the right position on the rope. Their role is to share a vision about what they're trying to create together. The leader's role is to help articulate *how* they are committed to pulling the rope together in unison and alignment. To lead actions and strategic plans that anchor the behaviors and structures that support the whole enterprise and mission.

The best leaders breathe oxygen into this mindset daily and their *thinking, acting, and interacting* remind us all that we are stronger together.

BREATHING OXYGEN

Is your team and organization inclusive, aligning everyone on the rope, and pulling in the same direction? What can you do as a leader to be more inclusive?

INHALE

- Include teammates in dialogue, development, and visioning.
- Widen the table to include more diverse backgrounds, ideas, and expertise.
- Make time to foster cross-organizational relationships and embrace authenticity.
- Ask clarifying questions to better understand another point of view or story.

EXHALE

- Siloed or elitist thinking.
- Talking about people who aren't in the room.
- Cynicism aimed to catch someone rather than help understand.
- Structures that exclude rather than include.

Notes

"Agility is principally about mindset, not practices."

—Jim Highsmith

CHAPTER 4

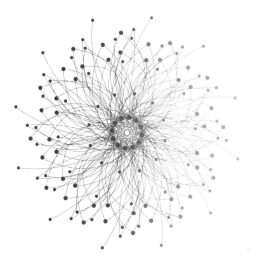

AGILITY
Possibility + Adaptability

Mental agility and the ability to let go of "the way we've always done it" in order to embrace opportunities and meet changing needs is the oxygen all leaders must breathe in the world we live in today.

3 Guys and a Birthday was one of the greatest entrepreneurial ventures you've never heard of—or so we say. Following my years and summers as camp counselors at the inspiring Camp Akita in Hocking Hills, southeastern Ohio, I joined my friends Gabe and Ben in a hilarious side hustle. We were in our twenties and hanging on to any opportunity to have more time laughing together and extending the summer camp experience into the other months of the year.

The idea was brilliant in its simplicity. Families would hire 3

Guys and a Birthday to whisk in and takeover a kid's birthday for two hours with customized games, skits, and laughter they had experienced at summer camp. It was a magical way for kids to bring a piece of camp into their life at home. From our first booked party to our last, it was a hit and a whole lot of laughs.

For each customized party, the three guys would come jumping out of a 1978 Volkswagen minibus. We would launch into the party in some costume specific to the theme, and the next two hours were jampacked with music and laughs. The three of us enjoyed making each other laugh and helping some kid feel special.

It was off to a great start, but after about five parties something became very clear. Our original vision of 3 Guys and a Birthday taking the kids' birthday scene by storm needed to be adjusted. As word got out through many of the parents about the success of these parties, we began being hired for more adult parties than kid parties. In a way, we were becoming adult entertainers (yes, in a different way). It was time to pivot, be agile in our thinking, and adapt to a new audience.

Next thing you knew, we were performing more adult parties than kid parties, and almost every single weekend was getting booked with a party for both Friday and Saturday night. The three of us were huddled around a table almost every Thursday night doing comedy writing in preparation for the *Saturday Night Live*–style skits we would perform to poke fun at the adult whose birthday we were celebrating. For one forty-nine-year-old's surprise party, we barged into the packed house wearing orange jumpsuits as if we had just escaped from prison. We began eating their food, making them laugh, and turning the party upside down. The whole time, the three of us were giggling about the path this enterprise was now taking.

The success of 3 Guys and a Birthday was fairly short-lived once we realized we really didn't want to be committing all of our weekends to this buffoonery (as fun as it was). I remember those days with great fondness and the mental agility it took to respond to changing opportunities. We relished the opportunity to adapt our efforts to connect with where this comedic experience was working.

OPPORTUNITYISNOWHERE

People see the heading above differently. Some clearly see that it says, "Opportunity is nowhere." Others clearly see that it says, "Opportunity is now here."

However you see it impacts your view. The power of our mind and the power of suggestion take us down different pathways. The mind will point us in a particular direction. We may just want to help train it in how we want to see the world.

Agility begins in the mind. It's "the ability to think and understand quickly." But we often need to practice how to breathe this way. It's way easier to cling to the patterns, routines, or "the way we've always done it." It takes practice to breathe in a new way.

The oxygen we breathe into a mind that welcomes change and adjustment is the beginning of being agile as a leader. Agile leaders then begin to see possibilities and breathe life into themselves and those around them about what is possible. Possibility that breathes life, excitement, and energy into all involved. And although agility begins in the mind, it flows into adaptability, which is the practice of adjusting our steps, actions, or courses of action. Adaptability is "the quality of being able to adjust to new conditions, to modify for a new use or purpose." Agility leads to possibility, which leads to adaptability. And it all begins in the mind. It all begins with the oxygen we breathe.

If you've ever watched an illusionist or magician perform, then you will better appreciate the power of the mind. They are masters at using sensory illusions, sleight of hand techniques, and trains of logic and memory to manipulate people's attention. Famous examples are when they make a ball or card appear from what seems to be thin air. Through master techniques that steal our attention, they are playing into the power of the brain to imagine and see what we have been trained to see or believe. What we give our attention to greatly affects what we see.

The same thing happens in our everyday lives. What we give our attention to greatly affects what we see. Our minds are powerful computers, capable of far more than we realize, but run on an unconscious "operating system," one based on easy, comfortable habits, routines, and ways of seeing things.

By the way, this serves us in many ways by helping us maintain routines, patterns, and structures to cling to in a fast-changing world. But it also limits us, because what we give our attention to greatly affects what we see. Our minds can become stuck in one way of thinking, acting, and interacting that is aligned with the illusion of what "we think we should see" rather than growing and expanding the ways in which we think, act, and interact. Leaders, teams, or entire organizations that get stuck in the "this is the way we've always done it" mode have often clung to those safe patterns rather than intentionally shifting their attention to try to see things differently.

Seeing possibilities and the ability to be agile and adapt the plan or path along the way take practice in the way we think, act, and interact. The recent global pandemic proved this and highlighted the effectiveness (and ineffectiveness) of leaders across industries and nations who were either able or unable to see possibilities, have agile minds, and adapt plans. The best leaders and team cultures in the world breathe oxygen into themselves and the people around them that stimulates new ways of thinking, seeing, acting, and interacting.

As Jim Collins pointed out in his book about companies that were built to last over many years, these companies create environments that preserve the very best of the core of their past and stimulate progress at the same time.

CONVERGENT VERSUS DIVERGENT THINKING

Leaders in the twenty-first century need both convergent and divergent thinking abilities and practices.

The term "convergent thinking" was coined by Joy Paul Guilford as the opposite form of what has become known as divergent

thinking. Convergent thinking generally means the ability ı
the "right" or "correct" answer to standard questions and th_ ᵤyᵖᵉ
of thinking that focuses on discovering the "single well-established
answer to a problem." Convergent thinking emphasizes speed, ac-
curacy, and logic, and focuses on the ability to recognize patterns
and recall familiar stored information.

Divergent thinking is the train of thought, process, and methods
used to generate creative ideas by exploring many possible pathways
and solutions to a problem. Divergent thinking methods are usually free flowing, spontaneous, nonlinear, and challenge the eyes
to see other possible solutions than the typical stored information
or habitual patterns.

Both forms of thinking are needed, and the best leaders and
cultures practice them both with their people.

We are living in the most highly distracted times in the history of the world for people, teams, and organizations. (Read my
book *ReMember: Renewing Our Memberships, Relationships, and Focus in a
Distracting World* for research on this topic.) Modern workers have
never been more busy, cluttered, distracted, or divided, and they
are feeling as lonely as ever.

Convergent thinking is practiced more commonly in today's
fast-paced world where, unfortunately, many team cultures
perpetuate "busyness" rather than honoring true effectiveness.
Speed-to-decision and activity are often modeled as most important. This perpetuates fast movement and quick decisions, but
not always the most effective, thoughtful, or creative solutions.
Leaders, teams, and organizations that get stuck in this mode
of operating can become so quick to find the first solution that
they continue to repeat the same patterns. They run the risk of
not being able to see other possibilities and have the capacity to
be agile and adapt.

Both types of thinking are needed.

Divergent thinking cultures and methods are not the only answer and not without their own challenges. Some can become so
enamored with the search for creative solutions and possibilities

that they get "paralysis by analysis" and can fall into the trap of never deciding or picking a solution. In these cases, progress is stymied by the inability to select a path and get to the work of execution and implementation.

Both types of thinking are needed.

The most influential and effective leaders, teams, and organizations in the world breathe oxygen that stimulates both types of thinking. They breathe oxygen into their divergent thinking to seek possibilities and also their convergent thinking to select the path, decision, option, and solution to pursue. In the midst of this highly distracted and busy era, the best leaders carve out time to breathe oxygen into divergent thinking with their people. They create space and practice to divert their attention to see other possibilities. They breathe oxygen into possibilities.

Then, with just the right timing, in an art form that is the essence of leadership, they transition the group out of divergent thinking into convergent thinking. They breathe oxygen that helps the group converge on the best solution and authentic path for their mission. They then breathe oxygen into the next actions that will stimulate progress down the path they've discovered.

FOUR STAGES OF THE CREATIVE PROCESS

Graham Wallas's 1926 book, *The Art of Thought*, introduced one of the first models of the creative process. Through research and study, he identified the four stages of the creative process: preparation, incubation, illumination, and verification. Since then, many have argued that other stages exist, including setting your intention from the beginning and leaving room for corrections and adjustments along the way. Wherever you fall in that discussion, creativity is a process.

It's easy to lose sight of the fact that creativity is a process like every other development process. Someone can carry with them a false narrative that creativity is just about the one idea, the spark, the one magical moment. They see the singer on stage performing, the comic in a crowded bar, the artist doodling on the street corner, or the witty friend who says something clever, and they think, "They are so creative." It's easy to continue the narrative that they just have something you don't have or that they can summon creativity on a whim.

The reality is that many of those individuals do have a unique, innate gift. They actually might be inherently more talented than you (and me). But what the false narrative loses sight of is the hours of preparation, incubation of the idea, illumination, and practice of the passion before the artist onstage even tries to verify it with an audience. The comedian Chris Rock spoke about his process, the many hours of writing, and the countless number of small clubs where he tried out his bits before he was ready to unveil his art. He would try the jokes out on small stage after small stage, always learning and adjusting his delivery, until they had been tried and true and were ready for the big stage of *The Tonight Show* or David Letterman. The path of creativity is much longer and wider than we typically acknowledge.

This is where I'm reminded of and get interested in bamboo. Hang with me. I've been fascinated by this image ever since I learned about it during the creative process of writing my first book, *Step Back from the Baggage Claim*. I became fascinated with how bamboo grows. If you've ever stood in front of a field of bamboo, then you know that on the surface it just looks like the bamboo shoots straight up from the earth in a straight line.

What I didn't know was what was occurring below the surface. Bamboo begins its growth from what is referred to as a "culm" within the soil. The bamboo begins to grow sideways underneath the surface. After it grows a little bit, it changes direction and shoots off in another direction, then another direction and another. All under the surface. Finally, when it's "ready," the bamboo changes direction one last time and shoots directly up through the ground. That is the visible, linear shoot. We see the straight bamboo sticking right out of the ground, but we miss the many turns and changes beneath the surface, preparing itself to be seen.

ative process is a lot like the growth of bamboo. So if we
athe oxygen into ourselves and others to practice a mind-
lps us see possibilities and become agile and adaptable,
then we need to create space to grow. Leaders need to make space
for divergent thinking to take place. We need to build in space to
think, dream, create, try, and let ideas emerge. Then, when they
are ready and we can see the solution, it's time to converge and
get busy bringing it to life and verifying the art.

REMOTE WORK

Every time I finish a virtual engagement with a team spread out
across the globe or a virtual keynote for an entire association
or organization, I'm grateful that these tools of technology exist.
Recently, I was with an organization with members spread out
across the United States, Canada, Europe, and Asia. We were able
to see each other, hear each other, connect, and align around
their mission, vision, and values for the culture they are creating.
It truly is amazing.

That said, I know it's not perfect. As I've been saying all along
during the pandemic, there is power in congregating. It's almost
impossible to create remotely the energy in a room where all people
are physically in the same space, aligning their minds and hearts.
In-person events and team gatherings are essential and will be
essential into the future.

Recent events have caused us all to experience some "forced
innovation." We have been forced to find new ways to innovate,
problem solve, and connect. This has led to revelations that perhaps we don't need to be on an airplane every week for a sales call
or drive six hours weekly for the one-hour meeting. We can be
more strategic and intentional about when we plan our in-person
contacts (because they will always be critical). We now can ask the
questions about how to leverage technology and virtual tools more
effectively (because it's smart).

With many of the companies and organizations I serve, we are looking at development and engagement strategies. We are strategically looking at the monthly, quarterly, and yearly in-person gatherings that are essential, and we can't afford to miss fostering relationships, developing leaders, and aligning culture. We are also asking what weekly, biweekly, and monthly meetings can be more effective virtually.

Some of the biggest complaints (or potential threats for long-term sustainability) I've heard from clients and research across companies with remote workers has to do with how we're adjusting to new modes of operation. Some experience the feeling that "the workday never stops because I'm always at work," because we're "stacking virtual meetings on top of virtual meetings." Screen fatigue sets in, and it's hard for employees to know when to turn work on and off. Employees also experience that many leaders and organizations are still learning how to best utilize the content of a virtual meeting differently than when you're in the same room with your people. They report that the majority of the content is "report outs" or updates. The content is boring, and the feedback many companies hear from their people is that virtual meetings just feel like someone is talking at them rather than with them. This leads to people who feel disconnected, lonely, disengaged.

This feedback and trends highlight that there are tremendous opportunities to better engage our people. Because of the quick switch that many teams and organizations made to remote workers to keep things afloat and maintain operation during challenging times, many teams and organizations are still getting the hang of how to engage in these environments.

The length and style of virtual meetings, and the creation of intentional connection and space for relationship building, are all things that have room for improvement. Virtual is just different, but it still can be effective. I know it's not the same as sitting in the same space and looking at each other directly (I prefer it too), but I have also been a part of some amazingly effective and impactful virtual meetings. Leaders need to continue to get intentional about how they lead their virtual meetings and create opportunities to breathe oxygen into their team members. It means we must get out of the typical "reports" or "updates" virtual meeting settings where participants are just sitting behind a screen and listening. We cannot just give death by PowerPoint or Excel spreadsheet sales updates. Whether utilizing in-person, virtual, or hybrid meetings, the most compelling leaders will be the ones who practice breathing oxygen into their meetings in more impactful ways. They make time to build connections. They will build in conversations that are the currency for change that engages the minds and hearts of their people. They will rally people around the compelling mission, vision, values, and strategy that point out their windshield. They will help their people participate in cocreating the culture. The proactive ways leaders adapt their old ways of operating and show agility with how they engage the minds and hearts of their people (both virtually and in person) are the key to the future of work. Employees and team members will begin to see possibilities for the road ahead. They will begin to see opportunities to grow as individuals and as teams. This will all occur as leaders adapt their mindset to better breathe oxygen into their people.

Inclusivity and alignment matter. Alignment begins with conversations that are the currency for change. Alignment allows the next conversations to be possible. Alignment is critical to reach your desired culture. *All* must be aligned on the rope and pulling in the same direction.

Then, breathing oxygen into our minds and into actions that bring agility and adaptability to life is key. Albert Einstein, the German-born American physicist and Nobel Prize winner, once said, "To raise new questions, new possibilities, to regard old problems from a new angle, requires creative imagination and marks real advance in science."

Victoria Swisher, author of *Becoming an Agile Leader*, points out, "With the growing and changing demands in business today and in the future, a person who possesses mental agility will be increasingly valued as a creative and resourceful problem solver in the organization. A healthy skepticism of favorite past solutions keeps the mentally agile mind open to new possibilities and fresh connections."

The 3 Guys and a Birthday idea or equivalent in your life and work may be playing out right now or in your new future. Will your eyes be able to see the new possibilities? Will your mind be agile enough to adapt to the new opportunities that are emerging?

We need to breathe oxygen that helps us see possibilities, adapt our path, and converge on solutions. The oxygen we breathe must help our minds be agile enough to have the energy to adapt to new opportunities that are in front of us.

**What kind
of thinking
do you
inhale,
and what
do you
exhale?**

BREATHING OXYGEN

In what ways do you and your team need to practice agile thinking and adapt to changing conditions? What new opportunities exist?

INHALE

- Identify new possibilities and more than one right answer.

- Consider ways in which your processes, structures, and mode of operation could improve.

- Make room to explore divergent thinking ideas before converging on the next steps for progress.

- Remind each other that there will be adjustments along the way.

EXHALE

- Rushing to judgments.

- "That will never work" thinking.

- Honoring policy more than results.

Notes

"Grit is sticking with your future day in, day out, and not just for the week, not just for the month, but for years."

—Angela Duckworth

CHAPTER 5

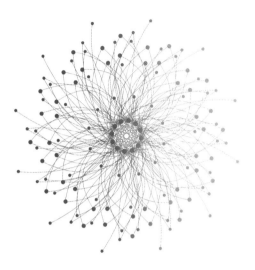

GRIT
Resolve + Toughness

Creating, achieving, performing, delivering, and leading anything of significance requires grit. The most compelling leaders and cultures breathe oxygen of resolve and toughness that sustain people on the journey. Sometimes we need to be reminded of the feats of others to be reminded of the grit and resolve that we're capable of. This story is one of those reminders.

The burgeoning, early-morning sunlight inched down the massive, seemingly flat surface referred to as the Dawn Wall—the famous three-thousand-foot granite rock face of El Capitan, the behemoth monolith in Yosemite National Park. Rock climbers Tommy Caldwell and Kevin Jorgeson hovered 1,200 feet in the air in their base camp portaledge (think hanging cot) suspended from the side of the rock face. The forty-mile-per-hour winds swirled.

They were in the middle of attempting to free-climb the Dawn Wall in a section in which that had never been done and to do it in one push. (Once they started, they would live on the wall.) There was no telling whether the feat itself could even be accomplished, or how many days or weeks it would require them to live hovering on the wall. They were two of the most accomplished rock climbers in the world but were attempting something nobody had even thought to try.

If you haven't seen the Netflix documentary about their story, *The Dawn Wall*, harness yourself in for an exhilarating and mind-boggling experience. After a full year of scouting and planning their path on the wall, and then years of practicing segments of the wall, they began their push from the bottom of the rock face. The conditions in winter were brutal. Living suspended in the air for nineteen days was grueling physically. The mental challenge was larger than the mountain.

Their passion bordered on obsession. Their commitment, resolve, and toughness were undeniable. Each inch of their journey up that three-thousand-foot climb is hard to even wrap your mind around. They just kept going. They were laser focused on the next grip, hold, or move that was right in front of their face, and they had to live and breathe each moment.

Tommy Caldwell, regarded as the greatest climber in the world at the time, knew he couldn't do it alone. He needed a partner. He needed to literally get on the rope in the climbing sense, but also metaphorically get aligned on the rope together with his new teammate. When asked about the experience, Tommy, in his humble and soft-spoken spirit, calmly said, "We all have an idea where our limits lie, but our perceptions are almost always off. We are capable of so much more than we ever know."

As I think you're picking up on, their story of commitment, grit, passion, resolve, and toughness is almost unbelievable. And therefore it can almost be written off as unrelatable. But don't tune out because of that.

I'm not a professional rock climber, and I'm guessing you aren't either. We all still need to digest their story and have the opportunity to glean lessons for our own lives. Most of us don't wake up hovering from a three-thousand-foot wall and attempting something that has never been done. But the oxygen they breathed, the mindsets they practiced, and the examples of grit, resolve and toughness are something we need to sit with. I need to sit with.

Leadership in the world today requires grit.

The most compelling teams and cultures have commitment, passion, grit, resolve, and toughness running through their veins. They aren't perfect. They aren't without challenges. They have off days. But they have a current of purpose, passion in their blood, and a resolve and toughness to their actions.

As you read this, you might be experiencing something in your life or career that feels like a daunting task or an unrelenting challenge. And if you aren't experiencing that right now, I bet you have in the past or know that someday you will. I can also guarantee that right now there are people on your teams, throughout your organization, and in your friend groups that are metaphorically climbing the wall. I know because I've met many of them, throughout hundreds of organizations over the last decade and beyond that I've been lucky to support.

I see team members trying to keep their job intact while trekking through a divorce, a loved one in the hospital, the heartache of a failed project or business, loneliness, systemic racism, social injustice, inequities in education, daily battles with mental illness, and so much more. The recent global pandemic has illuminated how much baggage so many people are carrying and the obstacles they are facing.

We all know the world has been difficult for many lately and has presented some challenges to all. If you need recent statistics, turn back to Chapter 1 of this book to be reminded. We don't need to depress each other or live in a place of doom and gloom. However, we do need to be honest about the challenges we're facing and realize the grit, resolve, and toughness that we all have within us to face them. We know through employee surveys that humans have felt as lonely as ever and that leaders and cultures can play a powerful role in their healing.

So yes, leadership in the world today requires leaders who can breathe oxygen into their own minds each day and breathe life-giving oxygen to the people around them. The most influential leaders in the world can't make the obstacles, challenges, and heartaches disappear, but they can walk beside and with people. Leadership and our commitment to each other are going to require grit, resolve, and toughness.

The opportunity is for leaders and organizations to become beacons of hope, care, support, and development, places where resources for people breathe life into them and others. I believe employers, leaders, and organizations are already, and even more so in the future, going to play a monumental role in mending, caring for, and supporting people and our world. Our places of employment have a tremendous opportunity and purpose right in front of us.

We need leaders and institutions who breathe oxygen into themselves and others.

REDEFINING TOUGHNESS

Let's start with redefining toughness. Along the way we need to make sure we're speaking the same language and defining terms in similar ways. I've talked about the word "leadership" needing to be redefined not as the person on top of the pyramid who barks out orders and tells everyone what to do, but as one who serves a mission greater than themselves and serves people. I've talked about the importance of understanding the term "culture" as a dynamic ecosystem of the way we think, act, and interact. And it's about time that we redefine the word "toughness."

Remember in elementary school when the "tough" kid was known as the biggest, strongest, baddest person on the playground? That's not toughness. In fact, as we all learned at different times after that, the people often thought to be "tough" due their size, strength, and "badness" were actually the softest. Toughness isn't about size and physical strength, although I know many tough people who are also big and strong. Some of the toughest people I know are not the biggest physical specimens. Toughness, in its most common definition, is the ability to "withstand great force without tearing or breaking." Toughness within people begins in the mind. Toughness, in the toughest people I know, begins in their mind and heart and grows outward. They have the ability to withstand great external forces without tearing and breaking and find a way to keep taking a step forward.

Mental toughness is the ability to endure, suffer, fear, care, be vulnerable, and respond by taking a step forward. Being tough is the ability to move into the next moment in your future with resolve to make it better. Even those suffering from mental illness are some of the toughest people out there. Pushing a smaller kid around on the playground isn't tough. It's easy. Stepping in front of the bigger kid to help the smaller kid requires toughness.

Every day, in our personal lives and places of employment, we need tough leaders who have the resolve to walk with people. Not tough by pushing people around and barking out orders, but tough by the ability to endure, suffer, fear, care, be vulnerable, and respond by taking a step forward with people.

It requires toughness to strive to be excellent at what you do. It requires toughness to be able to put yourself out there by making a presentation or challenging the status quo of your team. It requires toughness to admit you are hurting and to reach out to a teammate when they are struggling. It requires toughness to admit when you are wrong and choose to walk toward someone you disagree with rather than away from them. We have all had—and will continue to have—moments of toughness and weakness.

Leaders and teams who learn to breathe oxygen into themselves and others and practice a mental toughness that challenges all to walk beside and with each other exhibit grit and resolve for others. It is far easier to cut and run, ditch out, or avoid the challenge.

ghness calls us to respond and move toward a better future in
e present moment.

Jay Bilas, ESPN analyst and former Duke basketball player,
in his book *Toughness*, quotes Kansas basketball coaching legend
Bill Self: "The difference between tough and soft is simple . . .
soft is when you choose the easier path when the right path is the
harder one."

✳ THE BARRY-WEHMILLER EFFECT

In a 2014 TED talk in Vancouver, Canada, author Simon Sinek
(*Start with Why*, *Leaders Eat Last*, and *The Infinite Game*) brought a
mostly unknown manufacturing company from St. Louis into the
global consciousness. The company, Barry-Wehmiller, which of-
fers packaging-equipment solutions; corrugating, sheeting, and
paper-processing solutions; and flexographic printing, along with
other services, was feeling the effects of the 2008 recession.

They had lost nearly 30 percent of their orders seemingly overnight, and the company's CEO, Bob Chapman, and his board had
big decisions to make. They needed to save millions of dollars, so
they gathered to discuss layoffs and how to respond to the crisis.
After much dialogue and consideration of divergent, creative options, the leadership team aligned and converged on a plan.

Chapman announced the news to all their employees who were
awaiting the dreadful decision. Chapman refused to let anyone go,
and they had come up with a creative plan to meet the needs of
all. He announced throughout the company, "It's better that we all
should suffer a little than any of us should suffer a lot."

They devised a furlough program where every employee was
required to take four weeks of unpaid vacation, but everyone's job
would be safe. They could take the time off whenever they wanted
and didn't have to do it consecutively, whatever was best for them.
The company saved the $20 million it needed and boosted morale
at the same time.

As Sinek observed, "When people feel safe and protected by the leadership in the organization, the natural reaction is to trust and cooperate."

Internally, people who could afford longer time off began sacrificing and giving up an additional week or two to those who were struggling and couldn't afford the full four weeks off. The actions of the leadership team breathed oxygen into the entire organization in a way that nobody thought was possible. Their mindset and actions set the temperature for how they were going to get through the crisis and breathe oxygen of grit, resolve, and toughness to all. The leaders chose to endure the present challenges and suffering with a commitment to the future they were creating.

When leaders breathe oxygen into the culture in ways that are consistent with the values of the company and the temperature they aim to set every day, then trust, morale, and buy-in go up. And that is not because it's just a great strategy. It's because of authentic and compelling leadership. This is when the famous quote "culture eats strategy for breakfast" becomes clear to everyone.

To be successful at anything requires grit, determination, perseverance, resolve, and toughness. Nothing worth creating or performing or competing or developing is free from challenges, suffering, and pain. To love something means you will go through moments of extreme pain. To create something means you will wrestle with hours upon hours of frustration, disappointment, and doubt. To grow a culture of team trust and alignment will involve skeptics, challengers, and naysayers. To become elite, best in class, or known as "the best" at whatever you or your team or company does will require grit, resolve, and toughness that carry you through the obstacles that show up along your path.

The process is the work. The journey is the work. The clarity of mission, vision, and values is the work. The relationships are the work. The practice is the work. The implementation and execution of the vision is the work. And it will require leaders who breathe good oxygen into themselves and others to take the next step. Four breaths and take a step. Four breaths and take another step.

The mindsets that we breathe oxygen into allow us to excel in times of success, endure times of obstacles, and prepare us for times we can't imagine. Every person and team experiences challenges.

I'M DYING, BUT I'M NOT DYING TODAY

My mom was five feet, three inches tall—if you count the few inches of hair poof she had on top of her head. She was tiny, but she was absolutely tough. My whole life, I watched her stand up for things she believed in, work diligently and consistently to see anything through, and take a stand on an issue even when it wasn't going to be popular. She was tough.

She had an amazing ability to sit with you and help you realize you were capable of more—not in a negative way, but in a truthful and honest way. She was tough (not mean but loving) in ways that weren't going to let you bullshit your way out of something difficult or something you said you were going to do. I have many friends that recall a conversation or moment with my mom where they felt absolutely loved and cared for. She helped them realize they were capable of more and that she believed in them. It was frustrating at times, but it was a gift.

So, after years of battling through breast cancer and coming out seemingly stronger, but then being told she had brain cancer, we knew the next challenges had arrived. Our full family immediately swung into action to walk with her, try to remove as many obstacles as possible, and try to breathe oxygen into her and each other.

I'll never forget showing up to my parents' house a couple months into the new diagnosis of brain cancer. Things had been progressing rapidly, but still so many tests were being done, and there was hope in the air that this was just the next rough stretch of road to get through. She was sixty-nine years of age and had been a pillar of health in all other aspects of her life.

With her newly outfitted walker to help her navigate her way around—due to the cancer messing with her balance—we made our way out to their back patio to sit by her coveted garden and talk. My siblings and I had been in constant communication and were working on all details regarding communicating with doctors, insurance, caregiving solutions, and so on. We had been in strategy mode for weeks.

As we slid into our patio chairs and the late-morning sun peaked through the trees and warmed our faces, my mom began to speak. "J, I want you to know that I'm dying," she began. The thickness of that moment and the heaviness of those words dropped right in the space between us. I couldn't believe those words were being uttered, and the tears began to roll down both our cheeks.

"I'm dying, but I'm not dying today."

She was sending a message and breathing oxygen into herself and me. She was being honest and vulnerable while admitting that she knew where this was heading for her life. And in the very next breath, she was communicating that she wasn't going to let this rob us of the moments we still had. Class was in session again, and the lesson was about gratitude and grit and seizing the next moments we had together.

It was one of the most gut-wrenching and powerful moments of my life. With the sun on her face and a smile that appeared through our tears, she was showing her gratitude and appreciation for that very moment. She was teaching again in the way she knew how to do. She was going to be honest about what we were facing, but she was choosing to embrace each moment she had. She was breathing oxygen into the mindset that was going to carry us through the final months of her life.

Even as I type this with tears in my eyes again, I'm flooded with images of the last seven months of her life and the grit, resolve, toughness, and love she showed us all. She shared openly and honestly about how she was doing, but always with the spirit that "she was dying, but not dying today." She had us roll her in a wheelchair across grass fields to sit on the sidelines of her grandchildren's little league football games. She boarded an airplane for a one-day trip to be present for her grandchildren's theater performance in

Kenosha, Wisconsin. We carried her up and down the stairs at a cottage on Lake Erie in Ohio so she could enjoy final moments of a last vacation with family.

Her toughness wasn't about being the biggest or physically strongest. And even as cancer attacked her brain, she was so mentally tough with how she approached each moment with love, grit, and resolve. She showed us again that toughness was about facing hard realities with a mindset that this moment is about building a better future. That was all she was in control of. She was dying, but she wasn't dying today.

In the final weeks of her life, as she was bedridden and unable to speak too much due to the energy it required, she still found moments to continue to teach us. At just the right moment of visitors' tears, moments of silence, or ends of days, she would say to us quietly, "All is well."

All is well with me and in the world. She was comforting us that she was okay. She was reminding us that we would be okay. She was breathing oxygen into us one last time. Our challenges, obstacles, and suffering will not define us. Our love and spirit will.

All is well.

IMPRISONED PHYSICALLY, MENTALLY, OR BOTH?

I have been visiting a death row inmate for the last couple of years. For anonymity's sake, I'll refer to him as Derek.

When the first set of bars locks behind you in a prison, it's hard to not feel a bit of your breath being taken away. Then you enter through four more areas of locked security blocks as you make your way back to the death row visitation section. Each slamming of a new section of gates behind you is jarring.

The first time Derek and I met each other, his giant frame—six feet, four inches, about three hundred pounds—seemingly took up the whole room. He had armed guards on either side as they walked him into the visitation room. His ankles were chained together, as were his wrists. They stayed that way during our entire visit.

We had only exchanged secure emails to this point, but a hug and looking each other in the eyes seemed helpful to us both. We hardly knew each other, and I couldn't help but think what a unique moment this was in our world.

We had to start from the beginning with each other. I was there with no agenda other than to just be with him. I had been connected with the prison through my church, but I was very clear from the beginning with him that I wasn't there with any agenda. My purpose was only to sit with him, to talk, and hopefully be someone in the world that would look him in the eyes and call him by name. Because Derek had to formally "accept" me as a visitor ahead of time with the prison meant that he had to desire to be visited by someone. I learned very quickly that I was the first visitor he had come to see him in over three years. The gravity of that set in with me.

He then started where he felt he needed to start. Why was he on death row? He went into the story from decades earlier as a young man and being caught up in a world of drugs, intimidation, and bullying people for money. He recounted the fateful night when, in a drug-induced state, and in the role he had been assigned due to his size and stature, he was talked into robbing a convenience store. With heavy and sincere eyes, he told of running out of the store that night and firing shots backward as he ran out the door, only hoping to scare people from chasing him, not trying to end anyone's life. The convenience store worker lost their life that night, and Derek's life moved behind bars. On death row.

I don't know the full story. Only Derek does, or those who were there that night. I don't have a need to know all the details. It's an awful situation, and it's hard to know what justice truly looks or feels like in a situation like the one he describes. My heart aches for the family who lost a loved one due to senseless violence. My heart aches for all who experience a nightmare like this in the world.

I was not there to tell him what he did was okay. I was not

there to preach to him about what he should have done or should do now. I was there to just be with him and let him know that someone in the world still saw him as a human being and was there to listen. It's that simple. I certainly don't have the rest figured out. It's important for me to challenge myself to sit with discomfort and resolve to care.

But what has intrigued me from day one of our relationship, as well as through the other visits and many emails throughout COVID-19 when visitation was not allowed, is how he attempts to breathes oxygen into his own life now that his life is behind bars. He is contained to a six-foot-by-nine-foot cellblock fortress. His day-to-day life now is a master class in controlling what he can control each day. He cannot control what happened in his past, the decision by the judge years ago, the schedule of his days, and the food put in front of him. The only thing he can attempt to control is the area within the confines of his brain and the six-foot-by-nine-foot space around him. His daily mental health is dependent on the oxygen he breathes. Too much toxic thinking and his days become nearly unmanageable and a nightmare to be lived. He needs oxygen that lifts him up, helps expand his vision, helps him connect with the few people around him, and fills him with gratitude rather than despair. It's a daily battle to breathe. It's suffocating behind the series of locked doors and barred cells. He acknowledges that his mindset is everything for how he navigates his life in between those walls. Like all of us, he has days where his mindset carries him to see beyond his surroundings and his whole body is filled with oxygen. On those days, the oxygen flows to everyone around him. And he also recalls days he battles toxic thinking, negative storytelling in his own mind, and the inability to see anything but the bars that imprison him. On those days, it's hard to breathe and there certainly isn't any good air to give to others.

I can't help but feel more oxygen come into my lungs as I make my way back out of each section off of death row and back out the doors of the prison. The first time I felt the fresh air hit my face coming out of the prison (after being in there for four hours) was unlike any feeling I've ever had. I sat in my car with the windows down and just stared at the giant barbed-wire fenced area and mammoth stone fortress.

I couldn't help but feel a sense of gratitude for a life of freedom. I couldn't help but think about all the lives outside of the prison who had been impacted by violence and crimes. I also couldn't stop from saying a prayer for Derek and wishing him strength, courage, and oxygen to breathe. Even though he did an unthinkable thing years ago, I hoped my visit breathed good oxygen into his life. I couldn't help but see the faces of my wife, children, extended family, and friends and feel love and appreciation for them. I couldn't help but think about the random person I would see on my path next and how fortunate they are (whether they are conscious of it or not) to have the life they have outside of a contained fortress. I know personal choices and circumstances around us impact the path we often walk.

I think about Derek often. One of the reasons I do so, however, is because I know all people are imprisoned, not behind actual bars but by their own mindsets from time to time. We might not be physically contained but feel imprisoned in circumstances in life or work due to the toxic air we breathe, the external world around us, choices we've made in the past, or stories we tell ourselves in our own minds about what is possible or impossible in life. We are fortunate to not be physically contained behind bars and a concrete fortress, but I know many people who have shared about times in their life when they've felt imprisoned and trapped by their own mindset. They express feeling like it's hard to breathe and hard to see beyond the bars in their mind. Again, if 80 percent of our thoughts are negative and 95 percent are repetitive, identifying which bars are real and which are not is critical. The air we breathe either imprisons us or sets us free.

I empathize with anyone in the world who is struggling right now and is finding it hard to breathe in good oxygen that gives them the ability to have the resolve to move forward. I know there are people within our families, our teams, and throughout our organizations who need support with breathing good oxygen and with navigating their way beyond the bars in their own minds. As leaders and organizations, we have a tremendous opportunity to help breathe oxygen. It doesn't mean we always can solve every problem or remove every challenge we might face, but it does help us, and those around us, breathe a little easier. When there is a void in communication or too much silence, negativity, gossip, blame, and false narratives creep in. So leaders need to be even more intentional to help their teams fill the void with the opposite of those things. They need good air to breathe.

Derek, and all of us, seek good oxygen. It starts with the awareness of when we are breathing polluted air that begins to take our minds down pathways of negativity, blame, and false narratives about a future that has not been created yet. It's in those moments that we need to step back and breathe in good air. Air that reminds us of what we have to be grateful for (no matter how harsh the circumstances) and air that shifts our mind back to what is within our control. We can't control all of the external forces, but there are always elements that are within our control. It takes grit, resolve, and toughness. It takes mental precision to move ourselves from a toxic pathway to a more productive mental pathway. What is within our control? What response will we choose? Inhale the energy that comes from choice and empowerment, and exhale the toxins of negativity and blame. Breathe.

SEEK "LIVING AND BREATHING EXAMPLES"

It's powerful in our own minds and throughout our teams when we can point to living and breathing examples of grit. The human mind often needs to see something happen before it will believe it. So, when we see living and breathing examples like I'm sharing in this book, it becomes more real to us, and grit, resolve, and toughness become more accessible to us all.

Alex Smith was the quarterback for the Washington Football

Team in the NFL in 2018 when he suffered a horrible compound fracture to his right tibia and fibula in a game against the Houston Texans. Smith underwent seventeen surgeries, developed life-threatening sepsis from an infection, and had to wear a boot to combat his drop foot. During the daily grit and resolve of his rehab, which spanned well over a year, experts questioned whether he would ever walk normally again. When he not only walked again but ran out onto an NFL field to take another snap as a professional quarterback, he was a living and breathing example of grit, resolve, and toughness. When people hear stories about athletes like Smith, whose injury almost took his life the unreal becomes real.

When people hear stories of single parents putting one foot in front of the other during a nasty situation to care for all those around them, the unreal becomes real. When they hear of businesses that fail but dig back to sustainability, the unreal becomes real. When towns hit by natural disaster rebuild, the unreal becomes real. When the University of Virginia men's basketball team became the first number one seed in the history of the NCAA tournament to lose to a number sixteen seed underdog in 2018, they became a national laughingstock. Then they came back the very next season and won the national championship. The unreal became real.

Every human needs living and breathing examples of grit, resolve, and toughness around us. Every team must seek out and acknowledge those who are exhibiting it in their lives. Showing resolve and walking together with people breathe oxygen into everyone.

STILL LEARNING

I carry the words and memories of my mom, "I'm dying, but I'm not dying today," with me every day. I think about what they mean for how I live my life today and who I choose to be in the world. My mom wasn't perfect, and neither am I. I think about the grit, resolve, and toughness she personified, and I think about it within the context of the leaders, teams, and organizations I serve. I think about the challenges and opportunities that all of us face, and I'm reminded that we're all dying, but we're not dying today. There are things within our control, and we get to embrace the day that is in front of us and what we want to create together. We might feel imprisoned at different times in life, but thankfully, we aren't physically imprisoned.

It begins with awareness that we aren't imprisoned (literally) and is then followed up by the choice to not be imprisoned (metaphorically). It's become clear to me that the most effective and compelling leaders, teams, and organizations on the planet will be the ones who are committed to breathing oxygen into their people each day. And it will absolutely take grit, resolve, and toughness to breathe some days. It will require a choice to dig in with grit to make the most of whatever we have come together to accomplish. It will require a choice to be tough in ways that are loving, honest, and connected to the brighter future we are moving toward together. It will require us to choose to take four breaths and take a step, focus on the next move we can make, and have the resolve to see it through.

Leaders who breathe oxygen in these ways will engage the minds and hearts of those they are traveling with. And you know what? I'll bet every significant performance metric will follow. Not the other way around.

I'm dying, but I'm not dying today.

I'm not imprisoned.

I am free.

All is well.

BREATHING OXYGEN

In what ways does your team need to see your vulnerability and resolve? What do grit, toughness, and resolve look like in action in your culture? What mental bars are imprisoning you and your team? Who are the living and breathing examples of grit in your culture?

INHALE

- Define what toughness looks like to you and for your team.
- Be vulnerable and share where you are struggling, challenged, or feeling imprisoned.
- Identify the path forward and the next steps you will take to show resolve.
- Share thoughts of gratitude and the purpose for the journey you're on.

EXHALE

- Trying to bully people to get your way.
- Masking your fear with false bravado.
- Wasted energy and thoughts that are fixated on the problem rather than the solution.

Notes

"A wealth of information creates a poverty of attention."

—Herbert A. Simon

CHAPTER 6

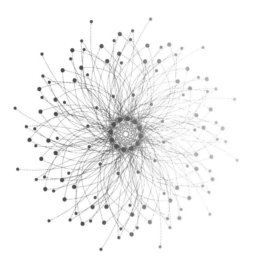

REST
The Secret to Elite Performance

The most compelling leaders and cultures in the next hundred years will be those who learn how to breathe oxygen that brings grit and discipline to skill mastery while also strategically allowing the body, mind, and heart to recharge along the way. The secret to elite performance is in the oxygen we breathe.

Rest of the mind, body, and spirit is one of the most ignored subjects in leadership and our team cultures. We perform better when we are rested. We are more effective at our individual roles when we are rested. We are better at aligning with our teammates when we are rested. We are more successful at hitting targets, maximizing our mission, and delighting customers when we're rested. We are also better husbands, wives, fathers, mothers, and friends. Rest actually makes us better at all we do.

However, we love talking about grit, especially in the United States. After all, hard work is the American way. We know and want to communicate to all that anything great is going to require extreme hard work, commitment, persistence, and grit.

I believe that. I've experienced that. I teach that. Just read the previous chapter. But it's only part of the story.

Breathing good oxygen into our minds and hearts is a combination of all the elements discussed in this book. The particles of good oxygen are part clarity of mission, vision, and values. Particles of inclusivity, kindness, and partnership. Particles of adaptability and agility to see new possibilities. Particles of grit, resolve, and toughness, and particles of personal and collective ownership that leads to action. All those elements create the life-giving energy and hope that fuel our thinking, acting, and interacting in the world. That's why we're talking about these mindsets in this book.

But there is one element that we have never been all that good about talking about, encouraging, and modeling for those around us. In some ways, we might be scared that people will take advantage of it or stop performing all together. The idea of *rest* to many seems soft or unnecessary. The "I'll rest when I'm dead" mentality is sexier.

We need a better relationship, understanding, and association with the concept of rest. I'll say it.

THE PART OF THE "10,000-HOUR RULE"
THAT GETS LOST

The 10,000-Hour Rule is talked about in almost every organization on the planet. It is referenced in keynote speeches, team meetings, coaching sessions, trade schools, and more. It is leveraged to make the point that you have to put in the time and work to become elite in anything. It's not talent alone; it's hard work and dedication to your craft. Again, I believe that.

Malcolm Gladwell, an amazing author and thinker, made this phenomenon famous in his book *Outliers*. He explores what it requires to become the best in the world in anything.

Gladwell references a study done in the early 1980s in Germany by Karl Anders Ericsson, Ralf Krampe, and Clemens Tesch-Romer. The study, featuring world-class violinists, is the backbone of the hypothesis that to become world-class in anything requires ten thousand hours of deliberate practice. Since then, many journalists, reporters, and keynote speakers have outlined and celebrated the careers of sports legends, business titans, artists, and brilliant educators who have mastered their crafts through the ten thousand hours of deliberate practice. We love stories about people who became famous due to their deliberate practice.

One of the key distinctions in this discussion is "deliberate practice." It isn't just "busyness," which I've spoken about so often. It isn't just ten thousand hours of being around and biding time. It is ten thousand hours of focused and deliberate practice of a craft in order to become an expert.

The study is fascinating, and Gladwell, as always, is masterful at weaving the research into real-life examples that show the study in action. It's a captivating, affirming, and inspiring call to action to dive into whatever craft you are focused on in your life and career. Mastery doesn't happen overnight. It takes deliberate and focused practice.

But that wasn't the entire study. Thankfully, Alex Soojung-Kim Pang, in his book *Rest: Why You Get More Done When You Work Less*, points out other elements of the same study. The full study revealed that the equation for world-class performers is more than just the ten thousand hours of deliberate practice. That is a critical element, but it's not the full story.

The research found that world-class performance is achieved when ten thousand hours of deliberate practice is combined with twelve thousand five hundred hours of deliberate rest and thirty thousand hours of sleep. The real equation isn't purely burning the midnight oil of deliberate practice but is also about deliberate rest of the mind, body, and soul and recovery time with sleep. And for those of you keeping score at home, performance is *enhanced* coming out of rest and recovery rather than with a brutal practice schedule that never stops. This is a very important distinction, because this isn't the narrative we always hear or share across our teams and organizations. In many settings, we've come to treat busyness and frantic work as a badge of honor. We've honored busyness instead of effectiveness. We haven't truly honored world-class practices.

Did you know that, in 2019, Americans left a record 768 million days of vacation on the table with their employers? That equates to nearly $66 billion in lost, unused benefits. Leaders and work environments are either leading us to believe we can't possibly rest, or we've bought into the myth that the faster I run, the farther I get. Somewhere along the line, we aren't valuing the role that deliberate rest, recovery, and space to think and process play in our overall performance.

This is where the neuroscientists jump in too. Whereas many scientists have been debating whether the human brain is like a computer for decades, most do recognize the analogy makes sense in some ways. Gary Marcus, a professor of psychology and neural science at New York University, says, "There is no reason to think that brains are exempt from the laws of computation." So, just like your computer or phone, if you have eighteen different programs running at the same time, eleven different documents minimized on your screen, emails beeping every time a new message comes in, and a to-do list that is never ending, your computer isn't running as efficiently as it can. You aren't maximizing its performance. There is a reason why computer experts recommended you "defrag" the hard drive of your computer (a machine) periodically to keep your computer from running slowly or freezing up.

Therefore, our brains operate much more clearly and efficiently and are more productive when we allow ourselves time to power down and intentionally rest. The result is we actually become better at whatever we are doing. Not just from practice and not just from rest, but when they are deliberately wed together.

Athletes like Lebron James, Tom Brady, Serena Williams, Simone Biles, and many others are examples right before our eyes. They became world class not just because of their talent but because of many other factors too. To name a few, their undeniable commitment to their craft through deliberate practice, their investment into caring for their own bodies, and the rest and recovery that they've found to fuel them. How they train, care for, and "defrag" their system helps them perform when it's needed most. Bill Gates's practice of his personal "think weeks," where he takes two weeks a year to go away by himself to read, think, and dream, has become legendary. He swears that he comes back clearer, more energized, and focused on what's next. He's more efficient coming out of those times.

As I've experienced, observed, studied, and researched some of the most influential leaders, artists, musicians, and creatives in our history, I've seen the ways they incorporate deliberate rest in their routines. You see deliberate strategies for rest and recovery such as daily power naps, disciplined sleep patterns, dedicated vacation time, yearly visioning and planning retreats, and extended sabbaticals for deeper learning and strategic planning. You see the intentional ways they protect sacred time and space in their schedules to reflect, think, recover, and allow new ideas to emerge.

Unfortunately, there are also many examples of burnouts or obsessive and "busy" leaders who drive themselves and everyone around them crazy. Some people never "turn off" work and are sending and receiving messages at all hours of the day and night The obsessive nature of their pursuits takes a toll on their physical and mental well-being as well as their relationships. More times than not, for these people who are in positions of leadership, this obsessive pace is unsustainable and tends to lead to a crash for them personally, for the relationships around them, and for the project they're so focused on. Again, it doesn't mean our lives and pursuits won't require grit and hard work in order to succeed, but it does mean that our obsessions cannot strangle the good air we need to breathe.

Our world needs more healthy leaders. We need more oxygen.

24/7/365

I know that many of you are saying, "Yeah, that sounds great to become such a healthy and balanced leader, but when? How?"

The 24/7/365 world we live in is filled with high demands. Kids' activity schedules are now on steroids in many communities and seemingly never stop. We live in a time with a continuous news cycle, constant messaging, and ongoing social media presence. Demands have never been higher to produce things quicker and cheaper. All of this creates pressure and often makes it harder to breathe. There is often a disconnect from what we know we need versus what we are interpreting the world needs of us. Again, the purpose of this is not to say we don't need to work hard or lock in and execute. We do in order to stimulate progress for a mission greater than ourselves. But not at the expense of ourselves.

Psychologist Herbert A. Simon said, "A wealth of information creates a poverty of attention." With more and more information coming at us, we are becoming more busy, cluttered, distracted, and scattered in our performance. We are becoming less efficient in many ways and learning habits detrimental to our long-term health and the viability of our career and vision over the long haul.

You don't solve a maze by rushing through it. We need to step back. Take a deep breath. Give ourselves room to think, rest, recover, and dream. Then we have more capability to be world class in that craft we have been deliberately practicing. We have more energy for that project that is going to require a large amount of grit, resolve, and toughness to see it through.

In our attempts to breathe oxygen into mindsets that bring out the best in ourselves and others, we can't forget to take moments, days, and even extended times to just get away and breathe. Good oxygen sustains us and fuels us in ways much else in the world cannot. We need time to close out the countless programs, apps, and thoughts that are running in the background of our minds. We need to reboot.

BIORHYTHM

In the last few years, I have become more aware of and interested in the concept of biorhythms. I certainly have become more aware of my own unique biorhythm and acutely cognizant of the impact personal biorhythms have on the leaders and teams I work with. But, as with everything, let's make sure we define the term so we're speaking the same language.

Biorhythm is a pseudoscientific theory developed by Wilhelm Fliess in the late nineteenth century that became popular in the United States in the 1970s. The general idea is that our daily lives are significantly impacted by rhythmic cycles throughout a normal month. As is commonly known, the average female menstrual cycle is twenty-eight days, but Fliess's theory was that all people follow biorhythmic cycles from the birth based on the release of chemical and hormonal secretions. He identified a twenty-three-day physical cycle, a twenty-eight-day emotional cycle, and a thirty-three-day intellectual cycle. The hypothesis was that based on your unique biorhythm, there were different times throughout the month when you were high and low in each of those categories. Understanding your biorhythm and when you were high or low could help you better understand when you were equipped with the best energy for a particular task.

That's about as far into the science or research as we need to dive here, and I certainly recognize that there are many studies and proof papers out there claiming their stance on both sides of this concept. No hard evidence has been able to fully prove or disprove the concept of biorhythms. It's a theory.

Still, I've become acutely aware of my own daily biorhythm and observed this with the thousands of leaders I've worked with over the years. I'm not sure about the whole physical, emotional, and intellectual elements of the theory and how they manifest, but I have fully acknowledged the personal biorhythm I experience daily.

I know my most creative times are in the mornings. I know I'm an early riser and that the elasticity and creativity in my brain functions at a higher level during early morning until about mid-day. I know my energy takes a major dip around 2 p.m. (as many experience), and I usually get a second wind around 3 p.m. I don't need research, data, or proof to show this. I know this about my own body. I experience it daily. This may not seem revolutionary to you, but hang with me.

I know my wife, Amy, has a different daily biorhythm. She is not an early riser and needs more sleep than I do. She needs some breathing room in her morning to get her mind going and to not feel rushed. She would not say that her most creative times are in the mornings. She begins to feel her highest energy mid-to-late morning, and that lasts her through midafternoon. She begins to feel a lull around 4:00 p.m. typically, but then her second wind kicks back in around dinnertime and carries into the evening. She has always been a night owl. That's more her natural speed. That's her unique biorhythm she feels daily.

Some of these can certainly be anchored by habits and routines we've gotten used to over many years, but much of this is just a natural state that has always been our unique orientation. Other leaders whom I have asked to track and observe their own bio-rhythms have come to similar conclusions. Some have been able to flip their habits and routines to the rhythm they more desire or need to be effective, and many have realized how to better leverage their own unique biorhythm.

Why is this significant?

A foundational element of emotional intelligence is self-aware-ness. Emotional intelligence is all about being aware of our own feelings and the feelings of those around us, and the ability to regulate our behavior in response to the temperature we want to set. As we become more aware of our own rhythms as a human being, we are able to be more intentional about what we give our energy to in more thoughtful ways. Better awareness and intentionality lead to greater alignment of our energy, focus, and effectiveness with a particular task or opportunity.

I'll personalize it again. As I became more aware of and

intentional with my own biorhythm over the last decade, I have been able to be more thoughtful about how I plan my daily and weekly schedule to maximize my energy levels and ability to focus. I don't schedule creative time to happen midafternoon, because that would be a disaster. I block time to make sure I am aligned to be successful with the corresponding task or function and natural energy level needed. I block early-morning time for all creative endeavors. These include writing, speech design or delivery, facilitation prep, important client meetings, and creative ideas to stimulate progress in my life and work. I utilize the late morning to early afternoon in my day, when my energy typically dips, to focus on office tasks that don't require the same level of creative energy. These include returning emails, scheduling, business forecasting, and the items on my list that just need to get accomplished without much thought. I'm an avid believer and practitioner (when I'm able) in the 2:00 p.m. brain reboot. I've been blessed to be able to (and have practiced) the art of the "power nap" by closing my eyes for twenty minutes to allow my brain to rest, reboot, and refresh. I know this is difficult for many, but I swear by it. My eyes open back up at the sound of my phone alarm, and I feel a renewed energy rather than limping to the end of my day. Sometimes I actually fall into a brief sleep mode, and other times my eyes, brain, and body just rest. My mid-to-late afternoon is reserved for face-to-face coaching meetings, other client support, and potential client calls. The mid-to-late afternoon has the perfect energy for me to be focused intently on the person I'm sitting with or talking with on the phone or computer.

I can't tell you how much more natural and productive my days feel when I'm able to align the tasks and functions to the right time of day for my energy. I'm more productive, helpful, passionate, and fully alive at the right level for the right thing. The key is connecting the right priority with the right people at the right time.

It has helped the communication and rhythm with Amy as well. As much as I'd love to take a walk first thing in the morning with her, that isn't the right rhythm for her. First thing in the morning isn't the right time to enter into serious thoughtful dialogue. We're learning how to better align the conversations, joys, tasks, and fun we have together in better alignment with both of our unique biorhythms.

Each time I take a leader or entire team through exercises that have them step back and analyze their own unique biorhythms, the response is extraordinary. For such a simple thing, many haven't taken the time to think about it. We just fall into the patterns of the way things are done or how we think we're supposed to do it. And for teams to step back and look at the rhythm of when they connect and how they attack their visioning, planning, and communication as a team is powerful. You often can't align the perfect rhythm for everyone on the team, but every team is able to be more thoughtful in their strategy, which leads to greater focus, alignment, and productivity.

From the rest and a recharged body, mind, heart, and focus, we are able to bring the right energy to the plan and actions needed next.

THREE-MONTH ACTION PLAN

Understanding your own unique biorhythm and being committed to strategic and deliberate rest will help enhance your performance and work/life balance. Like everything though, it doesn't just magically happen, you have to intentionally plan it. I also prefer the mindset that pushes aside the traditional "Long-Range Plan" formula utilized by many leaders and companies in the past for a more realistic "Long-Range Vision + Short-Term Plan" approach.

Let me explain. What I don't believe in is the arduous process that so many teams and companies have entered into, creating binders that chart every "i" they are going to dot and every "t" they are going to cross in the next ten years. So many places have entered into this process and then those binders sit on a shelf and collect dust. I do not believe in that.

What I do believe in is the exercise of creating long-term visions and short-term plans. Finding alignment with your people, your leadership team, your spouse, your family, or the board of your organization around a vision (where you're heading) in the next one, three and five years, is powerful (and critical for success). It is big picture. It is the 30,000-foot view of the landscape where you hope to travel. And it is okay that not every "i" is dotted yet or "t" crossed because, the truth be told, you don't know what's going to happen. And it is perfectly okay to admit it.

The world is changing so quickly that it is impossible for you to know every aspect of what will emerge on the path ahead. There will be things that are out of sight now that will appear later. There will be obstacles. There will be detours. And yes, there will be surprises and successes, too. The exercise of visualizing the direction you're heading is critical. It is life-giving. If it is a compelling vision, it will align and energize people. It will be oxygen.

From the long-term vision comes the short-term plan. I do an exercise with many clients that I call the *Three-Month Action Plan.* It helps them boil down their long-term vision into shorter, actionable moves. It helps them get clear on their own personal mission that will guide their performance for the next three months. It's their mantra, their focus for who they are striving to become.

We are living in the most distracted times in the history of our world. The Three-Month Action Plan exercise helps you concentrate on your top five priorities. I know we often want to jump from Point A to Point Z in one giant leap, but that never happens. We have to focus on going from Point A to Point B first. We must identify what success with our top priorities will look like at the three-month mark.

Precisely what are the first actions necessary to stimulate progress this week, this month, next month, and month three? What's the objective? What's the message? Who owns it? When will the action be put into place?

One action at a time, we set the temperature for the future we hope to create. The once scattered or inconsistent temperatures that we had been setting now become more consistent due to the clear vision we bring into existence. The culture begins to shift. The temperature in the room changes. Something is different, real. The once-distant light now is visible and shines brightly to everyone around us. It communicates that change is not only possible, but it is also happening. Now.

PULLING YOUR ENERGY TO POSITIVE

We know the path or plan isn't always smooth and without obstacles. Every team or group of people on the planet will encounter negativity. It does and will always exist. In fact, in some ways, the negativity reveals that we don't want something. Too much negativity becomes toxic. Negativity reveals to us that we want and need a different energy and is a symptom that can trigger a positive response. And when we are better rested and recharged, we're better able to navigate the negative energy.

This is when a friend of mine taught me how a battery works. On every battery, there is a positive and negative side. Both are needed in order to produce the power. The way that the energy gets transferred throughout the battery is when the electrons are pulled from the negative side to the positive side. That's right, the electrons are *pulled* from the negative side to the positive side, and this creates the energy that fuels whatever the battery is being used for. It's an important nuance (but powerful leadership image) that the energy is *pulled* from negative to positive, not *pushed*. Influenced, invited, and nudged forward rather than coerced.

Much like every individual person, let alone every team or group of humans on the planet, the most significant work we do is pulling ourselves from the negative to the positive side of our thinking. That is what creates energy for ourselves and for those around us. The most effective leaders and teams in the world are strategic, intentional, and deliberate about creating environments that pull the negative energy to the positive side. They breathe oxygen into efforts that pull the negative to positive.

Engaged cultures that are compelled by a future they are committed to creating, are filled with people who are enrolled in meaningful work that will move things forward. They buy in to the future they are trying to create. They understand that they too must put actions into motion. They must set the temperature for those around them. These types of leaders and teams know they must breathe oxygen into it to keep it moving, growing, and pulling in the positive direction.

You cannot control all the negativity or external conditions in the world around you. You cannot control the conditions within your industry or all the conditions within the marketplace you're apart of as a business. You certainly can't make all the negativity in the world disappear, but you can pull the negativity that is within your control to the positive side. You can be a steward for the small section of the world that you occupy and pull the energy in a different direction. There will be negativity that will rock you from time to time, but you are responsible for your energy. Your actions matter with the people and projects within your part of the organization. They set the temperature. They either breathe oxygen into pulling the energy in the positive direction or breathe oxygen into fanning the flames of negativity.

So, how will you recharge your energy? What direction will you pull the energy? What oxygen will you breathe?

BREATHING OXYGEN

When in your days, weeks, months, and year, will you deliberately rest to re-charge your brain, body, and passion? How will you shift your thinking about the equation for elite performance? What's your most effective biorhythm as a leader?

INHALE

- Take twenty minutes to close your eyes, rest your brain, and let it wander into sleep mode.

- Start your day with words of gratitude about the people and elements of your life and work that you are thankful for.

- Identify times that you will deliberately rest.

- Encourage others to shift their association with "rest" and the truth of elite performance.

- Make adjustments to your schedule that are within your control in order to align with your personal biorhythm.

EXHALE

- The "I'll sleep when I'm dead" mentality.

- Stacking up meetings all day long that leave little margin for reflection or action.

- Worries and fears that others will judge your time off. Focus on recharging you.

Notes

"Leaders create leaders by sharing responsibility, creating ownership, accountability, and trust."

—James Kerr

CHAPTER 7

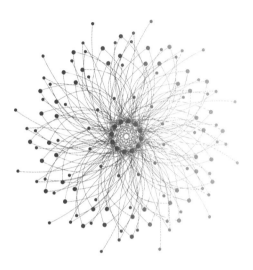

OWNERSHIP
Accountability + Action

Every single time someone follows through on what they said they were going to do, it breathes oxygen into the room and to everyone in the space. Positive accountability and ownership of our actions give energy and life to others.

Did you know that in the United States alone, nearly three billion dollars in lottery winnings go unclaimed every year?

Yes, unclaimed. Sitting there. Waiting. Never claimed. Three billion dollars.

The data tell us that Americans love playing the lottery. Over 50 percent of the US population plays the lottery regularly. A CNBC study found that the average American spends nearly $1,000 every year on lottery tickets.

Research shows that we love to play the lottery. We love the idea, the promise, the hope of winning. We are just awful with the follow-through.

It paints the picture that even when we win, many have already lost their ticket, forgotten to check the numbers, or just plain got distracted. And the money goes unclaimed, opportunity lost. If you're feeling a slight sickness in your stomach right about now, that's normal. Fortunately, to relieve a bit of that feeling, in most states, the unclaimed funds are used to support something good, whether that be education or state projects. So it's not a total loss.

This is just one of many odd examples of human behavior, but the reality is many humans aren't great with follow-through. Many people struggle with taking ownership and following up the intended idea, vision, hope, or words with action. I choose to believe that most are well intended (and that has certainly been my experience within many teams and organizations), but moving thoughts into action needs more support than we originally believed. Therefore, the leaders, teams, and cultures who are able to shift the mindset of their people into action through positive accountability and ownership are ones who bring out the best in people, and the results follow.

An ownership mindset means we take psychological responsibility and care for what we say and do. Items we say we'll do or commitments we've made aren't someone else's responsibility. An ownership mindset is not a temporary "rental" that doesn't get our best effort or energy. Our commitments are seen as ours to follow through on. An ownership mindset doesn't mean someone is perfect and doesn't make mistakes but that they don't skirt around or shift the responsibility to others. An ownership mindset and an ethic of follow-through can be taught, supported, grown, and rewarded.

RECLAIMING THE WORD "ACCOUNTABILITY"

We need a better relationship with the word "accountability." Unfortunately, it has taken on a negative association in the minds of many people because of the ways in which teams, companies, parents, and coaches have talked about the word over the years. The focus around accountability has leaned so far toward the items that don't get done that its meaning has been hijacked to mean the proverbial "slap on the wrist" or "accountability police" catching us doing something wrong. "I'm going to hold you accountable" has taken on a negative connotation that it only means holding you responsible for the things you don't do.

This misses one valuable side of accountability. It's blurring the true and compelling element and essence of the word accountability. Accountability simply means "the fact or condition of being accountable; responsibility."

It's not only the things you don't do, but it's also the things you *do* do. Accountability is not a negative term but in fact a very positive one. The problem has been that we only use the word or reference the idea when we are identifying an act or person who has not lived up to their responsibility. The opportunity and mindset shift needed within our teams and organizations is to reclaim the true definition and begin to use the word accountability in positive ways.

When an employee is on time and prepared for every meeting in a week, they have been accountable to their teammates and their duties. When a team member stops and acknowledges the performance or positive attitude of another team member, they are being accountable to the values they said they desire as a team. When a husband or wife takes out the trash upon the request of their partner, they are being accountable to the partnership they committed to. Every single day we perform many, many tasks and actions that represent positive accountability. We just don't recognize or acknowledge these efforts nearly enough. And we haven't seen them as "accountability." Then we "hold each other accountable" when we miss the mark on something. We need to practice both. When someone only hears that negative edge when someone "holds them accountable," then they begin to lose sight of all their other positive efforts. This often leads to lower self-value, erodes trust, and reinforces a negative association with the word accountability.

An ownership mindset within a team or culture means I'm accountable for me and you are accountable for you, and we are accountable for us. We want to breathe oxygen of positive accountability into all we do, because we sincerely want to uphold our end of the bargain. We understand that we each play a significant role in the health of the team, the relationship, the culture. Positive accountability is one of the strongest forces on the planet.

WE ARE ALL AMBASSADORS OF OUR CULTURE

A twenty-something-year-old came whizzing down the hallway on a scooter right past me. The walls were covered with memorabilia and relics from the early days of Southwest Airlines all the way up to the present. The second-floor patio deck overlooking the airfield was beginning to welcome a crowd of gathering employees at their headquarters in Dallas. I was lucky to be touring their facility and learning about their culture as part of an event that I was speaking at the next day in Dallas. Everywhere you walked, you felt like you were a part of something that was special and still in motion.

The poster was everywhere all over the building. In big words, it said "Count on Me to Own It" and was followed by the statement, "We are all ambassadors of our culture." Those words, and more importantly that feeling, was palpable throughout the building.

The day I was there was a lesson in their culture and a confirmation of everything I had been speaking about and supporting for years. They spoke glowingly about the ups and downs, twists and turns of their past as a company and lessons learned along the way. But in all their celebration of what was built in the years prior, most of their words and focus were fixed on the days ahead. Just because the culture had been celebrated globally through countless awards, praise from experts, and their own employees, the desired culture was still a work in progress. Even at a place like Southwest

Airlines, which has had so much to be celebrated for in the past, challenges and obstacles can always arise. All organizations have challenges and times that require them to align their people again.

They explained the example that if you wanted to work at Southwest Airlines, you were told from day one that they needed to be able to count on you to own it (the culture, that is), not rent it. New employees were expected to take psychological responsibility and ownership over the culture that was still being established. After all, we (all employees) are *all* ambassadors of our culture. They were committed to breathing oxygen into the cultural eco-system each day through dedicated and intentional mindsets and actions that begin with each individual. All own the culture. All are accountable. On good days and bad days.

The reality for all our relationships and teams is that the culture is never finished; each breath and action is cocreating the present moment. The ecosystem is living, growing, and morphing in this very moment by the way we think, act, and interact. The intentional breaths we take, mindsets we feed, and actions we put into place will send ripples throughout the entire ecosystem. And together, the culture is created and experienced.

The best leaders, teams, and organizations on the planet under-stand that their cultural ecosystem is one that needs continuous oxygen. The vision for the culture they are aiming to create into the future needs to be clear, the mindset of ownership needs to be embraced, and intentional actions, structures, and processes that support the growth need to be put into motion. They breathe oxy-gen into the culture by the way they hire connected to the culture they desire. They breathe oxygen into the culture by the way they onboard new employees into an ownership mindset. They breathe oxygen into the culture by training and developing their people on what the future culture looks like in action and behavior. They breathe oxygen into involving their people in development focused on the core values and what it means to become a culture ambassador. They breathe oxygen into their culture by catching, recognizing, and celebrating actions that bring their core values in the present moment rather than just at a once-a-year performance evaluation. They breathe oxygen into the culture by making time as teams to have conversations that are the currency for change when individuals or teams get off track or when something detracts from the ecosystem. When a person or team or area of the company appears to be experiencing a depletion of oxygen, energy, and focus, they think creatively to breathe oxygen into those in need. They own it. Accountability is a positive force. We all are ambassadors for the culture we're committed to creating together.

THE FIVE-TO-ONE RATIO

Did you know some researchers can predict whether a relationship is heading toward a divorce just by watching the way the couple interacts with one another?

For years, the Gottman Institute in Seattle has been studying relationships and the factors associated with strengthening the dynamic between partners. Their "research-based approach to strengthening relationships" has led them to many conclusions about what kind of interactions give life to a relationship and what kind of interactions strangle the growth. In other words, what breathes oxygen into the relationship and what steals oxygen from the relationship.

They have found that "the frequency and intensity of negative interactions (arguments and fights) was one of the strongest predictors for divorce." The research showed that in healthy relationships that are thriving and growing, the ratio of positive to negative interactions during a disagreement is five to one. Five positive interactions to every one negative interaction. That's the power of negative energy and interactions—it requires five times the positivity to balance it out. In unhealthy, debilitating relationships heading toward divorce or breakup, the ratio is 0.8 positive interactions to every one negative interaction. The conclusion of the study is that most relationships where one or both of the people are committed to winning the argument or getting their way are headed for destruction. The relationships where both people are committed to a shared vision and recognize their individual responsibility in cocreating meaning together leads to healthy realignment even in the midst of disagreement.

Douglas Smith, author and founder of the company White Pine Mountain, has been studying happiness for years. I sat with him for a cup of coffee years ago as he was releasing his first book and have enjoyed his work ever since. In a recent blog he wrote, he made an important distinction that I loved about the difference between discussion and dialogue.

In most normal conversations, the words "discussion" and "dialogue" are used interchangeably, but their roots are actually quite different. The word discussion comes from the Latin word *discussus*, the same Latin root for "percussion" and "concussion," meaning "to shake" or "smash apart." Discussion, as Smith pointed out, is by design a form of competition or combat between two or more people to see whose ideas or thoughts will prevail. All debate team competitors or those who appreciate the art of debate understand this nuance.

The word dialogue comes from the Greek words *dia* and *logos*, essentially meaning "flowing through." In dialogue, two or more people are seeking to build a pool of shared meaning so that an effective decision can be made. Both parties are coming together not to win the debate but to understand the other person and find a good path forward. Dialogue requires all people involved to come to the table with the desire to hear each other, seek understanding, return to the meaning and purpose of the relationship, and choose what to do next.

Leaders, teams, and organizations that take psychological ownership of and accountability for the relationships and culture breathe oxygen through healthy dialogue into their ecosystem. They are aware that the ratio between positive and negative interactions is at least five to one, and they make time for dialogue when disagreements occur. It doesn't mean that every decision is done by committee vote or that there aren't nonnegotiables or expectations of performance on the team. In fact, it means they are so clear about the expectations, core values, and commitment to the culture they are trying to build that it is easy to spot when they have individually or collectively strayed from the vision. The spirit isn't to win the war or argument individually but rather to work toward raising the bar to be the best, most authentic version of the culture they desire to be. The shared meaning of the team is bigger than the individual battle. A higher value is placed on collective intelligence than on individual intelligence.

WHAT WE ALLOW, LINGERS;
WHAT WE TEACH, TRIGGERS

I use this phrase in leadership development and culture-shaping initiatives all the time: what we allow, lingers; what we teach, triggers.

The words, behaviors, habits, procedures, policies, and actions that we allow, linger. As leaders, and throughout the culture, all of those things that are allowed end up becoming the culture that others experience. The words we choose, the behaviors that follow, the habits formed, and "the way we do things" become the ecosystem all experience. Often, without bad intentions, habits are formed, people cut corners, and the things we allow just linger within the culture. It's easier to just go on than to stop and teach something different. When things are allowed that are counter to the values of the team, the culture suffers.

What we teach, triggers. Every time we teach something that is in alignment with the team values, it triggers a positive chain reaction that spreads to others. The words and language we use drive behavior. They matter. The behaviors and actions that follow those words send a message that we follow through on what we say. They communicate that we mean it. The habits we form are directly connected to the things we've been taught. How you hold a pencil, shoot a basketball, drive a car, and participate in a conversation are a direct result of what you have either been taught and developed or not taught and what has just been allowed and lingered.

It's not about rigidity. It's about intentionality. It's about commitment, practice, and positive accountability toward a particular outcome. The most effective leaders, teams, and organizations in the world are proactive and intentional about what they are teaching. The words, behaviors, habits, policies, procedures, and actions are intentionally connected to the culture they are trying to create. Everything is taught, practiced, reinforced, rewarded, and celebrated in alignment with their cultural vision. If different actions, behaviors, and habits are being formed within their culture counter to what is desired, then it's not purely an indictment on the individual but seen as an opportunity for leaders to teach better or differently. Rather than just allowing undesirable behaviors, what will we teach differently? Awareness begins with recognizing what is being allowed that is counter to the values and then intentionally teaching a new habit or behavior. The intentional teaching will trigger a more positive chain reaction.

The culture is always changing.

The question is, what role are we playing in what it becomes?

What we allow, lingers.

What we teach, triggers.

CAMERON MITCHELL RESTAURANTS

At its height, Cameron Mitchell Restaurants had ninety different locations for its different culinary concepts across the United States. The company has weathered the pandemic and is back on the rise. It has won numerous culinary awards, and its people-first culture has helped bring to life its vision, "Great people delivering genuine hospitality."

Founder Cameron Mitchell has been a guest at my Thermostat Cultures Live event and joined me in dialogue about his company's rise in the culinary and hospitality world. Values, and constant teaching about and development of those values, have been instrumental in that rise. And as Cameron reminds us, "your associates have to see your values backed up with action."

He recalled a story at one of his restaurants on a crowded weekend night. The place was packed and humming with energy. The food and genuine hospitality were on point. However, one large table of ex-athletes had been getting increasingly lively as the night went on. The GM came to find Cameron and let him know that some of the female staff had reported crude comments and poor behavior by the guests at that table.

This was a teachable moment. Either something would be allowed to linger, or a message would be taught.

Cameron calmly approached the table and thanked the guests for coming in for the night. He then told them about the remarks and behavior that had been reported and let them know that was not going to be allowed at his restaurant. He calmly asked them to pay their bill and exit the restaurant.

The testosterone at the table—and the shock that the restaurant wouldn't want their clout or money to stay longer—led to some resistance. Again, without raising his voice, Cameron said, "Listen, this is my restaurant, and I won't let anyone treat my people with disrespect. So we have two options here. Either you calmly pay your bill and call it a night, or I call the police and they walk you out of here. We both want option A."

Finally, after more resistance, cooler heads prevailed. The entire staff was watching how this situation was handled and what went down. In a moment, all the talk about "associates come first" played out right before their eyes. As Cameron recalled, most restaurants or GMs would have the slogan "the customer is always right" echoing in their ears or would be afraid of losing customers. But he had been clear from the beginning that his company was here to serve their associates, who then served their guests. Not the other way around. The message was taught that night. Disrespect was not allowed to linger. A different lesson was taught and triggered a positive chain reaction throughout all his employees.

On the other end of the spectrum, Cameron shared about how

teaching this kind of thinking and values within the culture has led to empowering the associates to create magical moments of genuine hospitality for their guests.

When the call came in to one of their Molly Woo's restaurants late one Sunday morning, the associate receiving the call noticed a different tone on the end of the line. The caller quickly explained that their son, Zac, was in Nationwide Children's Hospital with a rare blood disease and was coming out of surgery soon. Their son loved the orange chicken dish, and they had been calling all around the city trying to find a place that was open that early on a Sunday where they could get orange chicken.

You see, orange chicken isn't on the menu at Molly Woo's. But the associate said, "Give me a few minutes and let me get back to you."

In a matter of minutes, the associate from Cameron Mitchell Restaurants called the family back to report that the sous chef was making the dish for Zac and that they would have it delivered to him, saying, "This one is on us; we are rooting for ya!"

The associates sprang into action to create a dish that wasn't on the menu and delivered genuine hospitality directly to the hospital where Zac was staying, and they didn't accept payment.

The values had been taught long before.

The ownership and actions followed.

"Culture and values are not something that's just up on our wall," says Cameron Mitchell. "It's a living, breathing entity. It's how we breathe."

WHEN ACTIONS VIOLATE VALUES (AND PEOPLE)

From the outside, many Americans might assume Fort Hood, the military base near Austin, Texas, to be one of the safest, most well-led organizations, with clear values and a strong chain of command. It turns out the command-and-control style of leadership only works in very few environments, and when values aren't lived, much damage can actually be done.

In December 2020, the curtain was lifted on a massive scandal that highlighted a culture of sexual abuse, intimidation, murder, cover-up, and information and behaviors that were just allowed to continue to happen. Over years, the report found a complete lack of leadership and a toxic culture far from the values most assumed were at Fort Hood's core.

The report came after the disappearance and killing of Army Specialist Vanessa Guillen, and the findings pointed to widespread abuse, distrust, and cowardice. Reports were ignored, pushed aside, and hidden. An independent review panel held 647 individual interviews, 503 of which were with female soldiers, and found "there was a fear of retaliation, all forms of retaliation, stigmatism, ostracism, derailing a career and work assignments," said the committee's chairman, Chris Swecker.

The committee identified ninety-three credible accounts of sexual assault, but only fifty-nine of them were reported, according to the report. They also identified 135 credible instances of sexual harassment, but only seventy-two of them were reported. Based on the findings in the independent review, the panel issued seventy recommendations to change the culture at Fort Hood. Fourteen leaders at Fort Hood were suspended or relieved of their positions.

"The problems that we saw are cultural, and everybody is involved in culture, from the highest levels to the one-on-one interaction between the squad leader and his or her squad member," said Jack White, a panel member who previously served as a law clerk at the US Supreme Court after graduating from West Point and serving as an active army officer and in the US Army Reserve.

What we allow, lingers.

Reports were ignored. Facts were hidden. Acts of retaliation and fear were allowed and sent the message that staying hidden was more valuable than stopping abuse. This isn't leadership.

This is surely an obvious and dramatic example of leaders who failed to live up to the core values of their group and allowed other behaviors to linger that were detrimental to their people. This is an abuse of power that led to a culture of abuse, lying, and assault.

Thankfully, and hopefully, those reading this now are not in a culture as scary as the one at Fort Hood. If you are, get out and get help. Those cultures are not excusable or acceptable.

Thankfully, the reality is that most of us don't live and work in cultures with these clearly toxic and abusive examples, but the reality also is that every culture has things that are allowed to linger that are counter to the things they teach. Many times, in small ways, words, actions, and behaviors lingering within cultures eat away at the very best the culture could be.

And let me make sure this is loud and clear, and you don't for a second hear me saying this as if I'm on a high horse talking down to people: all people and cultures are imperfect. None of us is perfect, and there is no perfect team or organization or company culture on the planet. All have flaws, and all have areas to improve and gain greater alignment with their people.

One exercise of alignment that is good to return to every once in a while is to identify honestly as a team or organization the words, actions, and behaviors that are being allowed that might be counter to the culture we want to create. What are we allowing to linger?

Then, what would we teach in order to set a different temperature and begin to shift the words, actions, and behaviors to better align with the culture we want? How can we breathe oxygen into our own development in these areas and help breathe positive oxygen into the others within our culture?

How will we own it next?

How will we be accountable to one another and help support each other in catching the best of our values in action?

What oxygen is needed?

IT'S NOT A DRIVE-THROUGH EXPERIENCE

I often tell audiences and clients that developing people and culture is not a drive-through experience. I know we often want everything in our lives to be freaky fast, but when it comes to leadership development with the people in your organization and shaping the culture you desire as a team, there are no quick-fix solutions.

That's why I talk about six As to the culture-shaping journey in *Thermostat Cultures* (assess, align, aspire, articulate, act, and anchor), because you can't accomplish everything all in one leap. Each step along the way plays a monumental role in what the culture becomes. Each step in the process and each moment requires us to breathe oxygen into it. The way that a spark becomes a flame and then spreads is by us breathing more oxygen into it. Feeding the culture that we want, together.

RINSE AND REPEAT

Leave it to Sprite or Mountain Dew or Coca-Cola or Pepsi to remind us of this. Marketers have been saying it for years. You may know the old marketing adage about the rule of seven. The concept is that someone has to hear a message seven times before they will act and buy whatever you're selling. In today's highly distracted world of continuous messaging, I'm guessing it actually is more than seven times. But for now, let's just go with seven.

I invite you to think about this concept beyond just selling a product or service. Think about it from the perspective of a parent, coach, department head, teacher, pastor, board chair, or anyone else trying to anchor important messages or teachings for a group of any kind.

We know this cognitively: you can't just say something once and expect it to stick. You can't just put a poster on the wall and say, "I told you so." You can't just send out one memo or email to the team and then cross it off your to-do list. You can't just say it once at your annual meeting and expect it to live and breathe within your people every other day the rest of the year. You've got to practice the rule of seven to anchor the important messages in your culture—over and over again.

For example, I often help organizations look at their onboarding experience and put more intentional anchors within their culture. We identify strategic ways to breathe oxygen into their people throughout the life cycle of their development and employment. If you only had five messages you could share with a new team member about the culture you're trying to create, what would they be? What's your plan to anchor those messages seven different times in the team member's first ninety days on the job? How will you breathe oxygen into those messages so that they are alive and growing?

The best cultures anchor their values and vision for the future within every element of their organizational story. It's the air they breathe. They support the messages individually and collectively. They take individual one-time actions and develop them into habits that slowly become "the way we do it here." Many small, intentional actions over time. They realize the rule of seven (and more) requires commitment and intentionality to breathe oxygen into the messages and development constantly. Rinse and repeat.

INVOLUNTARY VERSUS VOLUNTARY

Breathing is one of the few bodily functions that can be controlled consciously but is also done unconsciously. Breathing is often referred to as an involuntary response. Our bodies, fortunately, breathe without us consciously telling ourselves to do so. Involuntarily, our body kicks in to assist us when we are sleeping or focused on another task at hand.

We also know the power of a voluntary response and a voluntary breath of oxygen. We've experienced the power of deep breaths when we're feeling levels of anxiety and stress. We've felt the vibrancy of expanding our lungs and voluntarily catching our breath during times of rapid heart rates, exercise, or excitement. We've experienced the internal response that shifts when we close our eyes, shift our thoughts from fear to gratitude, and sit quietly. Our heartbeat and our mind slow down. Oxygen returns to all areas of our bodies. Voluntary deep breathing is also what athletes do before beginning a routine or competition. This strategy deliberately increases oxygen levels in the blood to improve athletic performance.

This book is about the voluntary ways that we can breathe good oxygen into ourselves and others. Proactively. It's about establishing pathways in our brains that allow us to fuel ourselves and others in life-giving ways. It is about bringing energy and fuel to the situations before us rather than suffocating the energy in the room.

While I was toward the end of the process of writing this book, I met Kim up at Lake Erie on the border of Ohio. From the moment I met him in passing, I had this strange feeling that we were supposed to meet. He was a short man in his seventies, with a beard, a ponytail coming through his hat, and colorful shoes. It was clear he was an artist. He had a soft way about him, and there was something I liked about him immediately.

As I later learned, he felt something similar about me after our initial three-minute conversation. The first encounter was focused on my new puppy. The second time we ran into each other later that morning, it felt like this wasn't a coincidence. We stood there together for the next thirty minutes and quickly learned why we had crossed paths.

He shared with me that he had recently been given a fatal diagnosis of idiopathic pulmonary fibrosis (IBF), a condition in which the lungs become scarred and breathing becomes increasingly difficult. It's not clear what causes it, but it usually affects people near their seventies.

Moments later, he asked me what I did for a living. We both had goosebumps emerge as I shared with him that I was in the final stages of this book, *Breathing Oxygen*. It was a sacred moment.

Kim went on to describe his daily mental challenges and his search for what helps him breathe better. He also described the way he and those in his life have helped him identify the things, situations, line of thinking, and stressors that limit his oxygen. He's acutely aware of what steals his oxygen.

Hope emerged toward the end of our initial encounter when he referenced another book he had stumbled upon, James Nestor's *Breath: The New Science of a Lost Art.* In the book, Nestor shares his research about world-record free divers who explore the ocean and can hold their breath between six and twelve minutes without coming up for air. Some of these divers have a lung capacity of fourteen liters, which is about double the size for a typical male. But as he points out in interviews, "They [divers] weren't born this way . . . They trained themselves to breathe in ways that profoundly affect their physical bodies."

The glimmer of hope was evident in Kim's eyes. "I just need to train myself how to breathe more fully." Our next conversation is already scheduled.

Our lives, and the ability to navigate all that comes our way daily, are predicated on our ability (or inability) to breathe oxygen that brings clarity, inclusivity, agility, grit, rest, and ownership to all we do. Our responsibility is to practice breathing oxygen into ourselves in these ways each day and each week so that we're able to also breathe oxygen into others.

Every single high-performing team, business, organization, school, church, sports team, family unit, or group of humans of any kind on the planet reaches higher results based on the air they breathe each day. Breathing is a conscious and voluntary act for them. They are committed to not just accomplishing the tasks before them but are diligent about how they breathe in the process. The air they breathe makes them better at what they do.

I'll personalize this again. I have no doubts that I am a better husband, father, teammate, friend, community member, and certainly a better partner to the teams and organizations that I support when I am breathing good oxygen. When my mind, body, and habits are working in alignment, I'm better at everything I do. When I'm running low on oxygen or breathing air filled with toxins of blame, negativity, excuses, and finger-pointing, then all of my performance suffers. I don't handle situations as well as I could, and I run the risk of damaging relationships along the way.

The way we breathe as leaders and the ways in which we practice breathing good, healthy, inspiring, action-oriented, and solutions-focused mindsets into our teams create the culture all experience. You walk into a team and it's felt. You walk into a meeting and it's palpable. You walk into a company and organization, and you can quickly see how the air they breathe is impacting their entire culture. The best cultures on the planet are proactive about filtering good air throughout all their spaces and helping to teach their people how to breathe together. And the results follow. They don't do it purely for the results; they do it because they want to authentically care for their people and create a meaningful culture. And in doing so, the results follow. They've gotten clear on the temperature they are striving to set as a team or organization and then choose to be committed to breathing oxygen into every step of the journey.

Lastly, I need to remind you that the temperature in your culture won't drastically change overnight. *But the temperature will shift.* Leaders throughout the culture will learn how to breathe oxygen into the room and strategically calibrate the thermostat. There will still be moments where it is too hot in the room or too cool. *But you'll recognize those moments with more clarity.* Some people will not understand the air you are trying to breathe or like the temperature you're trying to set, because they don't want to change. *But you will also find those who rise up to partner with you to move things forward.*

You cannot control everything in the external environment and world, but you do have a say in the air you breathe. What do you choose to inhale, and what do you choose to exhale? The oxygen we breathe to fuel our minds and actions helps us to maintain, grow, and develop the cultural ecosystem we want. As I've shared in *Thermostat Cultures*, we must be strategic as a team and organization for the steps of culture-shaping to calibrate our thermostat, but you need to sct your own thermostat first so that you are able to help others. You have to breathe good oxygen yourself first before you can help others. You might be a leader by title, but you are also a leader in the sense that someone is always watching what you're doing. They're taking their cues from you. The air will begin to shift your thinking, acting, and interac will spread to others. Your oxygen will give life and and others.

> "To laugh often and much; to win the respect of intelligent people and the affection of children; to earn the appreciation of honest critics and endure the betrayal of false friends; to appreciate beauty, to find the best in others; to leave the world a little better, whether by a healthy child, a garden patch, or a redeemed social condition; to know even one life has breathed easier because you have lived. That is the meaning of success."—Ralph Waldo Emerson

That's leadership. That's a winning culture that delivers meaning, care, and results. That's a culture I want to be a part of creating. The air we breathe impacts the quality of our life and work.

Breathe in. Breathe out.

Inhale what you need.

Exhale what you don't.

You'll be glad you did, and so will those around you.

Let's fill the world with good oxygen.

BREATHING OXYGEN

Who and what are you positively accountable for? How could you follow through more consistently to show more ownership? In what ways do you need to practice and own your breathing mindset?

INHALE

- Extend positive interactions to those around you, and assess whether you're experiencing the five-to-one ratio in your relationships.

- Identify the things you would like to teach more intentionally to trigger positivity.

- What messages and stories do you need to rinse and repeat with your people to share consistent oxygen with others?

EXHALE

- Address the bad habits, words, or behaviors that you and your team are allowing to linger within your culture.

- Let go of viewing accountability as meaning when someone doesn't do something. Shift the mindset to catching others doing things well.

Notes

"What is honored will be cultivated."

—Plato

ACTIONS THAT EXPAND OR DEFLATE

Inhale

CLARITY

- Establish clear language for the mission, vision, values, and strategy

- Describe roles, and express clear expectations

- Make time to connect as a team and to build key relationships to align clarity

- Inhale gratitude, celebrations, and appreciation

INCLUSIVITY

- Include teammates in dialogue, development, and visioning

- Widen the table to include more diverse backgrounds, ideas, and expertise

- Make time to foster cross-organizational relationships and embrace authenticity

- Ask clarifying questions to better understand another point of view or story

AGILITY

- Identify new possibilities and more than one right answer

- Consider ways in which your processes, structures, and mode of operation could improve

- Make room to explore divergent thinking ideas before converging on the next steps for progress

- Remind each other that there will be adjustments along the way

GRIT

- Define what toughness looks like to you and for your team

- Be vulnerable and share where you are struggling, challenged, or feeling imprisoned

- Identify the path forward and the next steps you will take to show resolve

- Share thoughts of gratitude and the purpose for the journey you're on

REST

- Take twenty minutes to close your eyes, rest your brain, and let it wander into sleep mode

- Start your day with words of gratitude about the people and elements of your life and work that you are thankful for

- Identify times that you will deliberately rest

- Encourage others to shift their association with "rest" and the truth of elite performance

OWNERSHIP

- Extend positive interactions to those around you, and assess whether you're experiencing the five-to-one ratio in your relationships

- Identify the things you would like to teach more intentionally to trigger positivity

- What messages and stories do you need to rinse and repeat with your people to share consistent oxygen with others?

- Consciously breathe oxygen into each room and every interaction

Exhale

CLARITY

- Scattered, confusing, and blurry communication
- Blame, gossip, excuses, and wasted energy
- Doubt, worry, and items out of your control

INCLUSIVITY

- Siloed or elitist thinking
- Talking about people who aren't in the room
- Cynicism aimed to catch someone rather than help understand
- Structures that exclude rather than include

AGILITY

- Rushing to judgments
- "That will never work" thinking
- Honoring policy more than results

GRIT

- Trying to bully people to get your way
- Masking your fear with false bravado
- Wasted energy and thoughts that are fixated on the problem rather than the solution

REST

- The "I'll sleep when I'm dead" mentality

- Stacking up meetings all day long that leave little margin for reflection or action

- Worries and fears that others will judge your time off. Focus on recharging you.

OWNERSHIP

- Address the bad habits, words, or behaviors that you and your team are allowing to linger within your culture

- Let go of viewing accountability as meaning when someone doesn't do something. Shift the mindset to catching others doing things well.

- Exhale the toxic air that is stealing oxygen from you and others

Breathe Oxygen into Your Team
Proactively Develop Leaders and Culture
Need a . . .
Team retreat?
Keynote speech?
Guide for your culture-shaping initiative?
Online program or distance-learning tool?
Emerging-leader or onboarding strategy?

www.JasonVBarger.com

Email Info@JasonVBarger.com to request
discounted bulk copies of his books.

@JasonVBarger on social media

Subscribe to *The Thermostat with Jason Barger* wherever you get your
podcasts.

RESOURCES

Baldoni, John. "Employee Engagement Does More Than Boost Productivity." *Harvard Business Review,* July 4, 2013. https://hbr.org/2013/07/employee-engagement-does-more

Barger, Jason. *Step Back from the Baggage Claim.* One Love Publishers, 2008.

Barger, Jason. *ReMember.* One Love Publishers, 2013.

Barger, Jason. *Thermostat Cultures.* One Love Publishers, 2016.

Behar, Howard. *It's Not about the Coffee.* Portfolio, 2007.

Biggest Unclaimed Lottery Tickets. https://www.lottery.net/articles/biggest-unclaimed-lottery-prizes

Bilas, Jay. *Toughness.* Berkley, 2013.

"Biorhythm." https://en.wikipedia.org/wiki/Biorhythm_(pseudoscience)

"Breathing." https://en.wikipedia.org/wiki/Breathing.

Brown, Brené. *Dare to Lead.* Random House, 2018.

CDC report on suicide. https://www.insider.com/cdc-11-percent-us-adults-seriously-considered-suicide-in-june-2020-8.

Davis, Seth. "Charming, Yes, but It's More Than That: How Gonzaga Built a Contender, and Has Stayed There." *The Athletic,* 2019. https://theathletic.com/1264670/2019/10/07/its-charming-but-its-more-than-that-how-gonzaga-made-itself-a-contender-and-has-stayed-there/

"Divergent thinking." https://en.wikipedia.org/wiki/Divergent_thinking.

Ferdman, Roberto. "The Chipotle Effect." *Washington Post, February 2, 2015.* https://www.washingtonpost.com/news/wonk/wp/2015/02/02/the-chipotle-effect-why-america-is-obsessed-with-fast-casual-food/

"Fourteen Fort Hood Leaders Disciplined as Probe Finds 'Permissive Environment for Sexual Assault' at the Army Base." NBC News, 2020. https://www.nbcnews.com/news/latino/probe-launched-after-vanessa-guill-n-s-death-finds-permissive-n1250372

Gladwell, Malcolm. *Outliers.* Hachette Book Group, 2008.

Goff, Brian. "The $70 Billion Fantasy Football Market." *Forbes,* August 20, 2013. http://www.forbes.com/sites/briangoff/2013/08/20/the-70-billion-fantasy-football-market/#14e5368a41b7

Harter, Jim. "Historic Drop in Employee Engagement Follows Record Rise." Gallup. https://www.gallup.com/workplace/313313/historic-drop-employee-engagement-follows-record-rise.aspx.

Haydon, Reese. "Show Me the Money: The ROI on Employee Engagement." DecisionWise. https://www.decision-wise.com/show-me-the-money-the-roi-of-employee-engagement/

Howes, Lewis. *The Mask of Masculinity.* The Gottman Institute, 2017, p. 52. Smith, Douglas. WhitePineMountain.com.

Marcus, Gary. "Face It, Your Brain Is a Computer." *New York Times,* 2015. https://www.nytimes.com/2015/06/28/opinion/sunday/face-it-your-brain-is-a-computer.html

Montini, Laura. "The Positive Power of Your Team's Darkest Days." *Inc.* https://www.inc.com/laura-montini/how-you-can-actually-boost-morale-in-your-companys-darkest-days.html

Mitchell, Cameron. *Yes Is the Answer! What Is the Question?* Ideapress Publishing, 2018.

"Oxygen." https://en.wikipedia.org/wiki/Oxygen.

Pang, Alex Soojung-Kim Pang, Alex. *Rest.* Basic Books, 2016.

Sethi, Lokanksha. "Social Media Addiction." Daze Info, January 12, 2015. http://dazeinfo.com/2015/01/12/social-media-addiction/

Suicide Rate and Divorce Rates 2020. https://www.insider.com/cdc-11-percent-us-adults-seriously-considered-suicide-in-june-2020-8.

Swisher, Victoria V. *Becoming an Agile Leader*. Korn/Ferry International, 2012, p. 59.

The Dawn Wall. 2015. https://www.dawnwall-film.com

The Social Dilemma. https://www.thesocialdilemma.com/the-film/

Ward, Marguerite. "Researchers Interviewed Executives from Google, KPMG, Microsoft and Discovered the 10 Guiding Principles That Make Work Meaningful for Employees." *Business Insider*. https://www.businessinsider.com/upenn-research-strategies-principles-meaningful-work-employees-2020-10.

Watson, Rita. "Embrace a Positive Mindset Backed by Research." *Psychology Today*, 2020. https://www.psychologytoday.com/us/blog/love-and-gratitude/202001/embrace-positive-mindset-backed-research.

"What Are the Stages of Creativity?" Interaction Design Foundation. https://www.interaction-design.org/literature/article/what-are-the-stages-of-creativity

Verma, Prakhar. "Destroy Negativity from Your Mind with This Simple Exercise." *Medium*, 2017. https://medium.com/the-mission/a-practical-hack-to-combat-negative-thoughts-in-2-minutes-or-less-cc3d1bddb3af.

ABOUT THE AUTHOR

 **Jason Barger** is committed to engaging minds and hearts in the world. He is a dad, husband, friend, chicken wing connoisseur, sports fan, and curious human.

Jason was recently celebrated as a Top 200 Global Thought Leader to Follow by PeopleHum and also recognized as a Top 20 Leadership Development Trainer by HR Tech Outlook. He's also the globally celebrated author of *Thermostat Cultures*, *Step Back from the Baggage Claim*, and *ReMember*, as well as creator of the Step Back from the Baggage Claim movement, highlighted by the *New York Times*, ABC News, *International Herald Tribune*, and many other outlets worldwide. His podcast, *The Thermostat with Jason Barger*, has been a hit.

As founder of Step Back Leadership Consulting LLC, Jason is a highly sought-after keynote speaker, facilitator, coach, and consultant, focused on leadership development, culture-shaping, and clarity of mission, vision, and values.

Prior to taking off to sleep in airports and observe human behavior, Jason led 1,700 people to construct 125 houses internationally for families living in poverty. As the former director of Camp Akita he also implemented the Streets Mission Project to serve the homeless in Columbus, Ohio. He is a graduate of Denison University, where he served as captain of the men's basketball team, and then received certification from Georgetown University in nonprofit executive management.

In 2004, he was one of five people in Columbus, Ohio, to receive a Jefferson Award, a national award given to "ordinary people doing extraordinary things." In 2014, he was a recipient of *Business First*'s Forty Under 40 award. Today, Jason and his family live in Columbus, Ohio. Follow him on social media @JasonVBarger.

To learn more, visit JasonVBarger.com.

3